# Confucian Moral Self Cultivation

學而不思則罔

思而不學則殆

*Study without reflection is a waste.*
*Reflection without study is a danger.*

Philip J. Ivanhoe

# Confucian Moral Self Cultivation

Second Edition

Hackett Publishing Company, Inc.
Indianapolis/Cambridge

10 09 08 07 06     2 3 4 5 6 7 8

Cover design by Abigail Coyle

For further information, please address

Hackett Publishing Company, Inc.
P.O. Box 44937
Indianapolis, Indiana 46244-0937

www.hackettpublishing.com

**Library of Congress Cataloging-in-Publication Data**

Ivanhoe, P. J.
    Confucian moral self cultivation / Philip J. Ivanhoe.—2nd ed.
        p.   cm.
    Includes bibliographical references and indexes.
    ISBN 0-87220-509-6 (alk. paper)
    ISBN 0-87220-508-8 (pbk.)
    1. Ethics—China.   2. Philosophy, Confucian.   I. Title.
BJ117.I8 2000
171—dc21                                                  99-052082

ISBN-13: 978-0-87220-509-3 (cloth)
ISBN-13: 978-0-87220-508-6 (pbk.)

The paper used in this publication meets the minimum requirements of
American National Standard for Information Sciences—Permanence of
Paper for Printed Library Materials, ANSI Z39.48–1984

# Contents

Preface                                vii

Introduction                            ix

1. Kongzi ("Confucius")                  1

2. Mengzi ("Mencius")                   15

3. Xunzi                                29

4. Zhu Xi                               43

5. Wang Yangming                        59

6. Yan Yuan                             75

7. Dai Zhen                             89

Conclusion                             101

Works Cited                            105

Index of Names                         118

Index of Subjects                      121

*For my parents, John J. and Dorothy A. Ivanhoe,*

*my wife, Jiang Hong,*

*and my children, Fu Sang (Carly) and Nuan Jiang (John)*

# Preface

This book is a revised and expanded version of an earlier work by the same title. The original work evolved out of a series of three talks presented on the fifty-fourth anniversary of the Rockwell Lectures, which I had the honor and pleasure of delivering at Rice University, in March of 1992. The theme of the lectures was Confucian moral self cultivation, and they were focused primarily on the thought of three figures: Mengzi ("Mencius"),[1] Xunzi, and Wang Yangming. The first lecture also contained material that forms parts of the *Introduction* and first chapter of the present volume. This material was substantially augmented and developed for the original publication. Chapters two, three, and five were essentially the lectures as given, incorporating minor modifications and with notes added. The fourth chapter on Zhu Xi and the sixth chapter on Dai Zhen were added. For this revised version of the volume, I have reworked all of the original material and added a new chapter on the Qing dynasty figure Yan Yuan.

The aim of the original lectures was quite ambitious. It was adopted as the guiding sensibility for my original work and remains the aim of the revised version: to provide a philosophically sensitive and sophisticated account of Confucian moral self cultivation, as represented by important figures from different periods of time, who presented distinct and diverse views. In particular, this book is designed to appeal to philosophically inclined readers who may have little or no knowledge of the history of Chinese philosophy, and historians and others interested in Chinese culture, who may have little or no knowledge of philosophy. With these aims in mind, I have endeavored to keep the technical vocabulary, both sinological and philosophical, to a minimum. However, where the special vocabulary of these disciplines was crucial to making a particular point, I have not hesitated to make use of these valuable tools and explain their special sense. Given the stated audience of this work, I have avoided secondary sources in languages other than English and philosophical works that would not be easily understood by novices. For those interested in pursuing more specialized issues relating to the topics examined here, the works cited provide a rigorous and thorough guide to this literature.

I have studied and taught the material that is covered in this work for many years, and the questions and suggestions of numerous colleagues, students, and other friends went into the original work as well as the current revision. Their criticisms and suggestions have helped me to think through these complex and fascinating issues. Among those who have made the most significant and direct contributions to the latest version of this work are Mark Berkson, Mark Csikszentmihalyi, Shari Ruei-hua Epstein, Eric L. Hutton, Paul Kjellberg, T. C. Kline III, Pauline Chen Lee, Joel Sahleen, Edward Gilman "Ted" Slingerland III, and Mark Ty Unno.

The University of Michigan's Center for Chinese Studies provided generous support for this project. Robert Rama provided a great deal of help in the preparation of the manuscript and also offered numerous helpful suggestions on its contents. Meera Dash offered careful and much needed editing and very helpful suggestions regarding the format and layout of the volume. I feel a special debt of gratitude to Deborah Wilkes, who encouraged me to undertake this revision and expansion of my original work and facilitated this endeavor in many ways. The support, criticism, guidance, and advice I received from these and others has helped me to improve the current volume significantly, and I hope that it proves worthy of their care and attention.

## Notes

1. Readers may be familiar with Mengzi through his Latinized name "Mencius," but in this volume I will employ the former. Similarly, "Confucius" is a Latinization of 孔夫子 *Kongfuzi* "Great Teacher Kong," but I will use his most common Chinese name, Kongzi.

*virtue → (de) how does it manifest?*

# Introduction

Before turning to the seven individual thinkers and their respective theories of self cultivation, let us begin by exploring the more general question of why the Chinese originated and maintained such an enduring concern with the issue of moral self cultivation. For while such a concern with self cultivation is by no means unique, the prominence that this theme has enjoyed throughout different Chinese traditions—Daoist and Buddhist as well as Confucian—is distinctive. For example, while certain western thinkers, notably Aristotle, were deeply interested in self cultivation, this was not as central a theme in the western ethical tradition taken as a whole. Western philosophers have been much more concerned with trying to define what the good is and worrying about how, if at all, one can come to know the good. Chinese thinkers have focused instead on the problem of how to become good. Moral self cultivation is one of the most thoroughly and regularly discussed topics among Chinese ethical philosophers. Why this is so is a complex issue. Parts of the account that I provide are admittedly speculative and to some degree the narrative presented here offers a cropped and idealized picture of a much more involved and extensive story. Nevertheless we can be confident that one very early notion—the concept of virtue—played a central role in the development of Chinese theories of self cultivation.

The story we are interested in can be traced at least as far back as the twelfth century B.C.E., the latter part of a period known as the Shang dynasty, and is recorded on animal bones and shells, that were used for divination, and ceremonial vessels and instruments of bronze.[1] In these inscriptions, we encounter an early form of a Chinese character that now is written 德 and which in the modern Mandarin dialect is pronounced *de* "virtue."[2] In these early contexts, *de* "virtue" was a kind of power that accrued to and resided within an individual who had acted favorably toward a spirit or another person. The favor shown could be some common act of kindness or in the case of a spirit the presentation of an appropriate sacrificial offering. It was believed that the recipients of such favorable treatment would naturally feel a psychic debt toward their benefactor and this feeling would, in turn, engender a desire to *bao* 報 "respond to" or "repay" the *de* "virtue" or "kindness" shown to them.

A related notion at the center of this cluster of concepts is another character, *de* 得 "to get" or "gain," which is etymologically related to *de* "virtue," phonetically, graphically, and semantically. One who has *de* "virtue" *de* "gets," i.e., "has some hold on" someone; virtue is a kind of power. In the context we are examining, it is specifically a power over

ix

others but one that, as we shall see, paradoxically cannot be used to manipulate others for one's own private ends.

In later, but still quite old sources, the notion of *de* "virtue" finds various but related expressions. These share the general sense that the *de* of a given thing is its inherent power or tendency and in particular its natural effect on other people and things. So, for example, we find passages in which a woman's sexual attractiveness is described as a manifestation of her womanly *de*.[3] A person or thing can have bad as well as good *de*[4] but in either case those who come within the presence of a person's *de* will be influenced by it—the nature of the influence often depending upon the character of the affected as well as the nature of the *de* involved. Across the different meanings this character has, *de* retains the sense of an inherent, spontaneously functioning power to affect others.

In the early oracle bone inscriptions, the notion of *de* is almost always found in contexts concerning rulers and had the sense of that virtue particular to a good ruler: royal virtue. Royal virtue enabled a king to accomplish a great deal but most importantly it enabled him to *de* "get" the endorsement of various Nature and ancestral spirits. Such support was thought to be necessary for him to gain and maintain his rule, for those spirits could—if properly induced—intercede on the ruler's behalf with the high god *Shangdi* 上帝 "The Lord on High," who ultimately controlled the forces of Nature and human destiny.

It is not altogether clear how one originally comes to possess royal virtue. It may be that virtue, at first, was something that *Shangdi* or *tian* 天 "Heaven" *ming* 命 "orders" or "decrees" for certain individuals. That a given person possesses virtue and is granted *tianming* 天命 "Heaven's Mandate" to rule, could simply be a matter of "fate," a meaning that the character *ming* had and still retains.[5] Or perhaps, even at this early stage in its history, *de* was thought to be something that one must earn through the accumulation of good acts. In any event, only a ruler who maintained a proper relationship with the spiritual world—and this entailed regular sacrifices and proper piety as well—could preserve his *de* "power" to rule.

With the emergence of a new ruling line, known to us as the Zhou dynasty, around the eleventh century B.C.E.,[6] the notions of *ming* "fate" and *de* "virtue" began to change.[7] A new sense of *ming* came into use in discussions about a king's ability to rule and the legitimacy of his rule. In such contexts, *ming* no longer had any strong connotation of "fate"; it came to mean the "Mandate (of Heaven),"[8] something a ruler could either earn or forfeit. An improper ruler, one who neglected his ritual duties, dissipated his *de*, while one who was scrupulous in his conduct preserved and could even augment his personal power. The king now was thought to have a moral and religious obligation to *jing* 敬 "revere" or "take reverential care of" his virtue. He did this primarily by paying strict attention to his ritual duties as king. These duties were numerous and varied, but underlying them all is the idea that the king must put the good of the people before the satisfaction of his personal desires. At times, the king might even be called upon to put himself at risk in order to benefit his people.[9] A king who failed to revere his virtue, by indulging his personal desires at the expense of his royal duties, would dissipate his virtue. His power would grow weak and eventually he would lose "Heaven's Mandate" to rule. In such a case, the *ming* "mandate" to rule would pass to another ruler or line who have demonstrated their moral worthiness to rule.

The Zhou rulers invoked the idea of a change in the Heavenly mandate to explain and legitimate their success over the preceding Shang dynasty, whose rulers they depict as profoundly self-indulgent and corrupt. They also used it to diagnose their own failures. For example, when the Zhou ruler was defeated by a coalition of local lords and border peoples in 771 B.C.E., it was interpreted as a testament to his personal moral failure. It seems that this particular king was fascinated with a lovely concubine named Baosi who took inordinate delight in having the king light the series of beacon fires used to summon his loyal vassals in times of attack.[10] To amuse Baosi the king had the fires lit on a number of occasions and his vassals dutifully rallied their armies and came to his defense. But after a number of such false alarms, they tired of this game, and when the real attack came, the fires were lit, but the call for help went unanswered. This ruler faltered and his rule failed because he put his own selfish interests before his role-specific duties as king.

The duties incumbent upon a king were defined by an increasingly explicit and complicated set of ceremonies and social practices known collectively as the *li* 禮 "rites" or "rituals." These included everything from formal, high religious ceremonies to the conduct of government and, as in the story above, included such things as one's personal deportment and behavior. Since everything the ruler did contributed, in some measure, to the character of his *de*, almost everything he did took on great significance. One can begin to see how the trajectory of this line of thinking leads naturally to a concern with moral self cultivation.

During this period, we see two related shifts in the Chinese religious and philosophical paradigm that were important for the emerging ethical consciousness. First, an appeal to kinship was no longer seen as sufficient grounds to legitimate one's rule. Heaven's Mandate was no longer simply viewed as a hereditary right, a question of fate. Rather, the right to rule was thought to depend upon the ritual propriety of the ruler.[11] But maintaining ritual propriety was not simply acting in a certain way; much more important was acting out of proper motivations.[12] Second, and this is critical, the virtuous disposition of the agent is what was valued—not simply the agent's overt behavior. These features of Zhou dynasty ethical and religious thought became central tenets of later Confucian philosophy and were developed with increasing sophistication as the tradition evolved. But the unmistakable precedents for these ideas can be seen in very early literature, such as the following passage from the *Zuozhuan*:

> The Duke said, "My fragrant sacrifices have been plentiful and pure. The spirits certainly will support me."
> [His minister] replied, "I have heard that the spirits in fact have no personal favorites but favor only a person's virtue. Thus the *History* says, 'August Heaven has no personal favorites; it only supports those with virtue.' It also says, 'It is not the sweet millet that is fragrant; bright virtue alone is fragrant.'"13

The idea that a kindness received has the power to induce the recipient to respond in kind continued to be an important aspect of the concept of *de* and contributed to the development and conception of what were to become key Confucian virtues. This mutual dynamic of *de* "virtue" or "kindness" and *bao* "response" was thought to be in the very nature of things; some early thinkers seemed to believe it operated with the regularity and force of gravity. At the very least, it was thought to be a natural and spontaneous tendency of human nature.14 In poetry of the period, we find examples such as the following:

> There are no words left unanswered,
> No *de* "kindness" left unrequited [without *bao*].15

In the case of the relationship between children and their parents, the felt "psychic debt" of the kindness received was thought, in principle, to be beyond the possibility of repayment and could only be addressed by cultivating and maintaining an attitude of thankful parental reverence or *xiao* 孝 "filial piety" throughout one's lifetime.

> Oh father, you begat me!
> Oh mother, you nourished me!
> You supported and nurtured me,
> You raised me, and provided for me,
> You looked after me and sheltered me,
> In your comings and goings,
> You [always] bore me in your arms.
> The kindness [*de*] I would repay [*bao*]
> Is boundless as the Heavens!16

The love and devotion one was to show toward one's parents was to extend even beyond their lifetimes, for one was expected to maintain sacrifices to them, as they took their place among one's ancestors, and continue to remember and revere their spirits. The power of their *de* extended beyond their lives, reaching out and influencing their descendants. But just as in the case of royal virtue, we see in later period writings an emerging attempt to ethically justify such practices. Just as one owed a good ruler deference and obedience because of his virtue, one owed one's parents reverence as an expression of the boundless love that one had received from them.[17] In both cases, it was thought that one would spontaneously feel the desire to respond in kind to the good that one has received and would take joy in so responding.

In the Zhou written records, the notion that a ruler with proper virtue has the power to attract and retain capable ministers and loyal subjects to serve him became increasingly prominent. Virtue was thought to exert a powerful influence over others that allowed a good ruler to rule without resorting to force. For example, in the *Zuozhuan* we find passages such as the following:

> The marquis declared, "Fighting with these multitudes, who can withstand me? What city could sustain their attack?"
> The reply was, "If you, my king, were to pacify the feudal lords through the power of virtue, who would dare not to submit?"[18]

This was roughly the state of things when Kongzi or "Confucius" came on to the scene. Together, he and his immediate followers began to form these ideas into a more coherent system of thought. Kongzi focused on and continued to develop the notion of *de* as a moral term of art. He emphasized and possibly originated the idea that anyone could cultivate their *de*. Moral self cultivation became the ideal of every *junzi* 君子 "cultivated individual."[19] *De* was seen as an endowment each person receives at birth, an inheritance one either cherishes and develops or ignores and squanders.[20] For Kongzi, *de* was less and less a matter of birth or one's relationship with powerful spirits.[21] Increasingly, it came to mean something like moral charisma: the natural attraction one feels toward morally great individuals, the same kind of feeling that people claim to have experienced in the presence of Mahatma Gandhi or Martin Luther King, Jr. However, *de* did retain a paranormal power to affect others. Kongzi believed that the virtue of a cultivated individual could sway the masses just as wind sways the grasses.[22] He believed that the "gravity" of a ruler's *de* attracts and retains good and loyal subordinates and subjects just as the north star attracts and holds the other stars in their orbits, circling around it.[23]

In the following chapters we will explore the process by which Kongzi and his later followers thought one could come to possess and develop *de*. We will see that they emphasized different and diverse aspects of this task and at times overtly and sometimes heatedly disagreed with one another about this central and critical issue. But we will see that they all believed one could fundamentally transform oneself, that such transformation was necessary in order to live an ethically satisfying and spiritually fulfilling life, and that it had the power to affect those around one in dramatic and profound ways. Thus the cultivation of virtue was of paramount importance for both self and society.

These different thinkers further believed that a transformation of the self fulfilled a larger design, inherent in the universe itself, which the cultivated person could come to discern, and that a peaceful and flourishing society could only arise and be sustained by realizing this grand design. Cultivating the self in order to take one's place in this universal scheme describes the central task of life for these and all Confucians and is the topic of the present study.[24]

# Notes

1. The best introductions to this period of Chinese civilization are: Kwang-chih Chang, *Shang Civilization* (New Haven, CT: Yale University Press, 1980) and David N. Keightley, ed., *The Origins of Chinese Civilization* (Berkeley, CA: University of California Press, 1983). For a more concise treatment that compares the development of early Chinese civilization with that of early Greece, see David N. Keightley, "Early Civilization in China: Reflections on How It Became Chinese" in Paul S. Ropp, ed., *Heritage of China* (Berkeley, CA: University of California Press, 1990): 15-54. For an edifying introduction to Shang oracular inscriptions, see David S. Keightley, *Sources of Shang History: The Oracle-bone Inscriptions of Bronze Age China* (Berkeley, CA: University of California Press, 1978). The most illuminating and thorough introduction to early bronze inscriptions is Edward L. Shaughnessy, *Sources of Western Zhou History: Inscribed Bronze Vessels* (Berkeley, CA: University of California Press, 1991).

2. The history of this concept is much richer than what I will present here. I am interested only in that part of its story which contributes directly to the issue of moral self cultivation. The best studies of the notion of *de* in early Chinese thought are Donald J. Munro's "The Origin of the Concept of Te" in his *The Concept of Man in Early China* (Stanford, CA: Stanford University Press, 1969): 185-197 and David S. Nivison's "'Virtue' in Bone and Bronze" and "The Paradox of Virtue," both in *The Ways of Confucianism: Investigations in Chinese Philosophy*, Bryan W. Van Norden, ed. (LaSalle, IL: Open Court, 1996): 17-43.

3. *Zuozhuan* Duke Xi, 24th year. See James Legge, tr., *The Chinese*

*Classics*, vol. 5, *The Tso Chuen*, reprint (Hong Kong: Hong Kong University Press, 1970): 192. See Nivison's discussion of this passage in *The Ways of Confucianism*, p. 33.

4. For example, in the *Shujing* we find expression like *xiongde* 凶德 and *e'de* 惡德 "bad tendencies." See James Legge, tr., *The Chinese Classics*, vol. 3, *The Shoo King*, reprint (Hong Kong: Hong Kong University Press, 1970): 244, 256.

5. One can see a vestige of this early world view in the modern Chinese word for "revolution," which is *geming* 革命 (literally: *ge* "stripping" the *ming* "mandate"). For a study of early philosophical senses of *ming*, see Edward G. Slingerland, "The Conception of *Ming* in Early Chinese Thought," *Philosophy East and West*, 46.4 (1996): 567-81.

6. The traditional date for the Zhou conquest of the Shang, 1122 B.C.E., now is generally thought to be wrong, though scholars disagree as to what the correct date is. David S. Nivison proposes 1045 in his "The Dates of Western Chou," *Harvard Journal of Asiatic Studies* 43 (1983): 481-580. David W. Pankenier argues for 1046 in his "Astronomical Dates in Shang and Early Chou," *Early China*, 7 (1981-82): 2-37.

7. For a concise yet incisive review of the evolution of the notion of *de*, see the entry "Tao and Te" by David S. Nivison in Mircea Eliade, ed., *The Encyclopedia of Religion*, vol. 5 (New York: Macmillan Publishing Company, 1987): 282-86.

8. For a good discussion of the emergence of this concept, see Herrlee G. Creel, "The Mandate of Heaven" in *The Origin of Statecraft in China*, vol. 1 (Chicago: University of Chicago Press, 1970): 81-100.

9. In his discussion of an oracle bone inscription dating from around 1200 B.C.E., David S. Nivison describes how a Shang king puts himself beneath or at risk before the spirits. Nivison says, "In this rite in which the king as diviner-intermediary assists another person to get well . . . because of his willingness to put himself in danger on behalf of another, his *de*, 'virtue,' is magnified." See "'Virtue' in Bronze and Bone," in *The Ways of Confucianism*, chapter 3. The same dynamic can be seen in chapter 20 of the *Analects*. There we see King Tang pronounce to the spirits, "If I in my own person do any wrong, let it never be visited upon the many lands. But if anywhere in the many lands wrong is done, let it be visited upon my person." Arthur Waley, tr., *The Analects of Confucius* (New York: Vintage Books, 1938): 231.

10. This story appears in the *Zhoubenji* chapter of the first official history of China, Sima Qian's *Shiji* 史記 "Records of the Historian." For an exploration of the legend of Bao Si, see Lisa Raphals, *Sharing the Light: Women and Virtue in Early China* (Albany, NY: SUNY Press, 1999).

11. While they accepted the practice of hereditary rule, early Confucians argued that virtue trumped heredity as a qualification to rule. They believed

and propagated stories about sage-kings like Yao and Shun who looked throughout the empire for the most worthy person to succeed them. It is also interesting to note that in these stories, the people they chose to succeed them were of remarkably humble origins. For examples, see *Mengzi* 5A5, 5A6, 6B15, etc.

12. Again, this idea gets stated most clearly by Mengzi. In *Mengzi* 4B19, Mengzi describes the sage emperor Shun by saying, "[He] acted out of benevolence and righteousness; he didn't just act benevolently and righteously."

13. From the *Zuozhuan*. The translation is adapted from Legge, *The Chinese Classics*, vol. 5, p. 146. For the two quotations from the *Shujing*, see Legge, *The Chinese Classics*, vol. 3, pp. 490, 539.

14. A number of early thinkers believed that the power of virtue and the dynamic of action and response extended beyond human beings and could be observed in a wide range of natural phenomena. Daoist thinkers, in particular, had a very broad conception of the range of its operation. For an exploration of early Daoist conceptions of virtue and a comparison of their views with those of early Confucians, see my "The Concept of *De* ('Virtue') in the *Laozi*" in Mark Csikszentmihalyi and Philip J. Ivanhoe, eds., *Religious and Philosophical Aspects of the Laozi* (Albany, NY: SUNY Press, 1998): 239-57.

15. From the *Shijing* "Odes." For the context of this line, see James Legge, *The Chinese Classics*, vol. 4, reprint (Hong Kong: Hong Kong University Press, 1970): 514. In another early Chinese philosophical text, the *Mozi*, these lines are followed by the couplet, "If you toss me a peach, I shall reply with a plum." For a translation, see Burton Watson, tr., *Mo Tzu: Basic Writings* (New York: Columbia University Press, 1963): 47.

16. From the *Shijing* "Odes." Cf. Legge, *The Chinese Classics*, vol. 4, reprint p. 352.

17. There is a clear asymmetry between what even the most filial children can do for their parents that is simply part of being the kinds of creatures we are. This goes beyond the mere fact that parents bring children into being (something some contemporary ethicists, who deploy a contractual model, discount because it is not an obligation children choose to enter into). While we might care for aged and ailing parents in something like the way they cared for us, we cannot support, guide, and inspire their growth as they did ours. Given this asymmetry, a distinctive feeling of reverence seems like a reasonable way to express gratitude. The case of a student and an important teacher is not altogether dissimilar and was regarded as analogous in traditional China. For an example of a contemporary ethicist who rejects any notion of filial obligation, see Jane English, "What Do Grown Children Owe Their Parents?" in Onora O'Neill and William Ruddick, eds., *Having Children* (New York: Oxford, 1979): 351-56. For a contemporary defense of filiality, see Christina H. Sommers "Filial Morality," *The Journal of*

*Philosophy* (1986): 439-56.

18. Adapted from Legge, *The Chinese Classics*, vol. 5, p. 141.

19. The equality of moral potential that Kongzi introduced is manifested in a variety of ways. For example, "The cultivated individual is not partisan, he follows what is right" (*Analects* 4.10). He studies to improve himself (12.5). Kongzi accepted any student, regardless of his status (7.7). And the cultivated individual's ultimate goal is universal moral brotherhood (12.5). For the classic exploration of this theme, see Donald J. Munro, *The Concept of Man in Early China.* Such equality of opportunity did not extend to women; however, a related though unequal set of feminine virtues can be seen in even the earliest writings. For a study focusing on the ethical state of women in early China, see Lisa Raphals, *Sharing the Light.*

20. In *Analects* 7.22, Kongzi says, "Heaven created the *de* within me."

21. In the *Analects* there is a clear reluctance to appeal directly to spirits for aid or support and a real concern for not patronizing the spiritual world. (See, for example, *Analects* 2.24, 3.12, 7.35, etc.). I do not interpret these passages as expressing a disbelief in spiritual beings but rather a rejection of a more magical conception of human-spirit interaction.

22. *Analects* 12.19.

23. *Analects* 2.1.

24. The task of describing this process is by no means limited to the individuals presented in this work, though they are some of the most interesting, distinctive, and influential representatives of this tradition. The leading spokesperson for the Confucian perspective in the contemporary world is Tu Wei-ming. For a concise statement of his contemporary reinterpretation of the Confucian vision, see his *Centrality and Commonality: An Essay on Confucian Religiousness* reprint (Albany, NY: SUNY Press, 1989). See also Tu Weiming, ed., *The Living Tree: The Changing Meaning of Being Chinese Today* (Stanford, CA: Stanford University Press, 1994).

孔子

# 1. Kongzi ("Confucius")

Kongzi (551-479 B.C.E.) was the first Chinese thinker we know of to work out the rudiments of a program for moral self cultivation.[1] The tradition he began is one of the oldest schools of moral self cultivation in the world; it is also one of the most enduring and influential.[2] But Kongzi did not regard himself as the *founder* of a school or movement or the initiator of a tradition; quite the contrary, he saw himself as the defender of a long-established lineage.[3] He once said of himself, "[I] transmit rather than create. I trust and delight in the ancients. . . ."[4]

Like almost every Chinese thinker of the early period, Kongzi believed in a past golden age, when sage kings ruled the world and all people lived in a peaceful and flourishing society. He believed that these individuals had devised a comprehensive family, social, and political system that harmoniously located individuals in a greater cosmic order.[5] Because their *Dao* 道 "Way" reflected a deeper pattern within the universe itself, it was regarded as the most "fitting" or "proper" way to be. At the same time, because it followed these natural patterns it proved to be the most efficacious, satisfying, and meaningful way to live.[6] Kongzi had taken it as his mission in life to preserve and propagate the records detailing the practices of these world-ordering sages.[7] These records served as the core of his program for moral self cultivation or *xue* 學 "learning."

There was much more to Kongzi's educational program than the intellectual mastery of these texts and technical facility in the rituals they contained; one was to *practice* and ponder these lessons in every aspect of one's life. Such reflective practice was thought to give rise to a synthetic understanding and intuitive sense of the Way. Kongzi believed that the process of mastering these rituals and the lessons contained in the classics was profoundly edifying and a source of great joy as well. The *Analects* opens with the line, "Is it not delightful to study and, at appropriate times, to practice what one has learned!"

As we shall see, later Confucians often argue about whether Confucian learning brings forth incipient tendencies of human nature or whether it provides a way to acquire a second, moral nature distinct from and to varying degrees in tension with one's natural tendencies. The next two thinkers we shall consider represent two extremes in this debate. Mengzi advocates a version of the first view, what I call a *development model* of moral self cultivation. His rival Xunzi proposes a version of the second view, a *re-formation model*. It is difficult to locate Kongzi definitively along the spectrum defined by these two extremes since he

1

does not directly tie his method of learning to a theory about human nature, as Mengzi and Xunzi do.[8] In his emphasis on the role of tradition and the need for prolonged and extensive study, Kongzi's original vision seems to have more in common with Xunzi's view. However, Kongzi's emphasis on the joy of moral learning, seen in the passage cited above, indicates that he saw human nature as more amenable to reform than did Xunzi. In this respect, he shows closer affinity with Mengzi's position.[9] I will describe Kongzi's position with an appropriately neutral term: as an *acquisition model* of moral self cultivation.

For Kongzi, the goal was not simply to become adept at performing the rituals and social practices of the sage kings and knowledgeable about the classics; he was not seeking simple rote learning nor was he promoting a set repertoire of behavior. He wanted people to use this knowledge and these practices to develop certain traits of character. He didn't just want children to know about filial piety nor even simply to act filially; he wanted them *to act out of* filial love for their parents. This requires one to have a cultivated sense of the overall aims and justification for filiality as well as an enhanced level of know-how concerning the ways to practice and promote filial virtue. He once said, "Nowadays, those who provide for their parents are said to be filial. But even dogs and horses are provided for. If there is no reverence—wherein lies the difference?"[10]

Kongzi not only wanted people to avoid the emotionally sterile and morally stifling perfunctory performance of ritual, he further realized that the virtues he sought to inculcate had no set form of expression. In unusual situations, the virtuous person might even act in ways at odds with or even contrary to what virtue would seem to require. Even under normal circumstances, the virtuous person is always fine-tuning the expression of virtue to fit the occasion and acting from the greater perspective of the overarching goals of ritual. No simple set of prescriptions will suffice to guide or describe such a person's conduct.[11]

In order for the system of ritual to result in the peaceful, flourishing society Kongzi envisioned, people had to use it to develop their own *de* 德 "moral charisma" or "power." This required them to reflect deeply upon the meaning of the lessons they studied and the rituals they practiced, not only to *xue* "learn" but to *si* 思 "reflect" as well. Kongzi expressed this ideal beautifully in a maxim, "Study without reflection is a waste. Reflection without study is a danger."[12]

There is a danger of misinterpreting Kongzi's call to engage in "reflection." For him, "reflection" is not ratiocination, in the sense of a logical process of deduction or demonstration that leads one to conclusions; *si* never means abstract, theoretical cogitation.[13] Primarily it means to keep one's attention focused upon and engaged with[14] something, often a goal or ideal which one intends to achieve.[15] Of course, Kongzi employed this sense of the word to direct people's attention toward *moral* goals and ideals, but the notion of focusing one's attention upon and longing for some desired person or object may well have been derived from an older, more general, usage. In one passage from the *Analects*, Kongzi quotes from a now lost ode:

The flowers of the cherry tree,
Constantly flutter and turn.
How could I not *si* "be thinking" of you?
But your house is so far away!

Kongzi goes on to comment, "He clearly was not thinking of her, [for if he had been] what distance would there be?"[16] This may represent the root sense of at least the philosophical meaning of *si*: to longingly focus one's attention on some object of desire. At the same time, *si* does appear to include relating such goals and ideals to one's attitudes and particular situation and hence includes a certain level of practical reasoning.[17]

In the passage just quoted, we see Kongzi drawing a *moral* lesson by unpacking the hidden meaning of an ode. This kind of interpretive exercise was an important part of his general system of education.[18] According to tradition, Kongzi is credited with editing an early collection of poems to form a book that is now known as the *Odes*. While most contemporary scholars no longer ascribe the editing of this text to Kongzi, the traditional view reflects the critical importance of this text for Kongzi and his disciples.

Kongzi did seem to believe that the *Odes* contained a hidden meaning that was at the very least consistent with the goals of moral self cultivation. He once said, "The *Odes* are three hundred in number, but one line from among them can cover them all, 'Oh! They do not stray!'"[19] We also have examples that appear to record Kongzi and his disciples teasing out the proper meaning of a particular ode by seeing how it applies to an issue concerning moral self cultivation.

Zigong said, "*Poor though without flattery, rich yet without arrogance,* how about that?"
The Master said, "That will do, but it is not as good as, *poor yet finding joy [in the Way], rich yet delighting in the rites.*"
Zigong replied, "The *Odes* say, 'Like cutting, like filing, like grinding, like polishing.' This, I suppose, refers to what you have in mind."
The Master said, "*Si*[20] I can now begin to talk with you about

the *Odes*. I tell you something that has gone before and you see what is to come!"21

This is a particularly interesting passage, for here we seem to have an example of a disciple proposing a maxim of the kind one can find throughout the *Analects*.22 Kongzi accepts the proposed maxim but improves upon it by offering another of his own design. The disciple then realizes that he was complacent in his interpretive (and by implication moral) efforts and needed to exert himself further. He expresses this with an appropriate passage from the *Odes* that taps into part of its hidden meaning—one should be ever-seeking to improve and further refine oneself.

Study of the *Odes* was just one method that Kongzi employed to help individuals develop the traditional virtues he espoused. Perhaps of even greater importance was practicing the *li* "rites."23 The "rites" which Kongzi advocated included not only grand religious ceremonies of state, but what we would call rules of social etiquette and standards of personal conduct as well. Practicing these rites played a central role in Kongzi's method of self cultivation: they shaped the character of those who practiced them, expressed and further refined the virtue of those who knew them well, and influenced those who participated in or observed a given ceremony.

Mastering these rites was a difficult and demanding task, and, as in the case of studying the *Odes*, as one's practice of the rites progressed, one came to have a deeper, more complex and complete understanding of their significance. The most profound truths human beings could know were embodied in these ritual practices and only one who could grasp their meaning could see these truths.

> Someone asked about [the meaning of] the Great Sacrifice. The Master said, "I do not know. One who knew its meaning could govern the world as easily as looking at this!" [He pointed to his palm.]24

As was mentioned earlier, the rites were not intended merely to elicit particular kinds of behavior, the goal was to instill certain sensibilities, attitudes, and dispositions in the practitioner. Kongzi believed that only the reflective practice of the rites could produce the particular set of sensibilities, attitudes, and dispositions needed for a harmonious, meaningful, and flourishing society. The rites achieved this first by restraining excessive behavior in a way that instilled an attitude of humility in the practitioner.

Yan Hui asked about humanity.[25]
The Master said, "To restrain oneself and turn to the rites is humanity. If for a single day one could restrain oneself and turn to the rites, the whole world would agree that one was truly humane. Does humanity not come from the self rather than from others?"
Yan Hui said, "May I inquire as to the details?"
The Master said, "If it is contrary to humanity, do not look upon it. If it is contrary to humanity, do not listen to it. If it is contrary to humanity, do not speak it. If it is contrary to humanity, do not do it."[26]

The notion that one must recognize that one's own desires are not preeminent, that an agreed upon and common set of rules takes precedence, is a prerequisite to participation in *any* kind of cooperative enterprise or game. Such deference to the larger enterprise is clearly needed for participation in society. The willingness to submit to mutually agreeable "rules" or forms of play is the beginning of one's sense of ritual propriety. Though Kongzi did not talk about the rites in quite this way, he did see certain gaming situations as paradigmatic examples of ritual propriety and opportunities for self cultivation. In particular, he appreciated the importance of athletic competition, perhaps because such competition required an enhanced ability to channel one's potentially violent and destructive energies in cooperative and constructive ways.

The Master said, "Cultivated individuals do not compete. [You might object by saying] don't they clearly do so in the case of archery? But before ascending [to shoot] they bow and defer to one another. And [after shooting] they descend and drink together. Such is the competition of the cultivated individual."[27]

In addition to this basic role of curbing our negative tendencies or vices, the rites also keep our virtuous tendencies within proper bounds. Perhaps Kongzi here had in mind the need to recognize and remember that harmonious relationships between people is the ultimate aim of and justification for moral self cultivation. If one loses sight of this aspect of the rites, one can mistake the task of moral self cultivation as primarily or exclusively a private, perfectionist concern, and this can lead one to run rough-shod over the needs, interests, and feelings of others. Such an attitude may give rise to the snobbery that infects crude and clumsy observances of etiquette, self-serving displays of power or prowess (disguised as true virtue), or an overbearing moralism.[28]

> The Master said, "Respectfulness without ritual becomes a burden to others. Care without ritual becomes timidity. Courage without ritual becomes disorder. Correctness without ritual becomes intolerance. . . ."[29]

The detail, care, and effort dedicated to the practice of the rites may well strike many modern western readers as archaic and oppressive, but perhaps this feeling will be less pronounced as one begins to understand the goal of this concern. For while Kongzi would not sit on a mat that was not straight[30] and was exceedingly scrupulous in his posture and demeanor, even when alone,[31] he was adamant in his insistence that these and related practices were not to be misconstrued as ends unto themselves. He believed that such apparently mundane details of life contributed significantly to the formation of one's character and that one must perform them in awareness of this fact.[32] In certain passages, the relationship between a given practice and its contribution to character formation is more obvious than in others. For example, the relationship is evident in the case of Kongzi not eating to repletion when in the presence of someone engaged in mourning.[33] On one level this practice simply expresses one's condolence to the mourner, but it also is meant to have a profound and direct effect upon the practitioner as well. It can bring to mind her cohumanity with others in her society, even those she does not know; it can remind her of the importance of her ties to family and friends and the fragility and transitory nature of human existence. It can also affect third parties who observe her practice and lead them to an awareness of their common fate and mutual solidarity as mortal human beings facing a threatening and at best difficult world. Properly construed, even such a simple practice can be seen as an impressive manifestation of humanity.

This concern with the details of life and the effects that they can have upon the formation of character is an important aspect of Confucian moral self cultivation.[34] Many of the things that Kongzi saw as *morally* significant tend to be viewed by modern western people as at best matters of *taste*. For example, Kongzi believed that music had a profound influence on the formation of character, and this led him to promote certain kinds of music[35] and argue for the prohibition of music that failed to meet his moral standard.

> Yan Hui asked about governing the state.
> The Master said, "Propagate the calendar of Xia, ride in the carriage of Yin, wear the cap of Zhou. As for music, let there be the *Shao Dance* [the succession dance of the sage emperor Shun]. Banish the music of Zheng and keep clever talkers at a distance. The music of Zheng is licentious and clever talkers are dangerous."[36]

The degree to which one finds this view objectionable, or even dangerous, might vary in light of the *kind* of music one is considering. It seems less controversial to claim that there is a standard for what is proper music on occasions like state funerals, presidential inaugurations, marriages, graduations, or college football games than for private listening. Kongzi was much more concerned with the former kinds of cases than the latter. Nevertheless, he would surely maintain, and it seems neither unreasonable nor untrue, that even in the latter cases, music has profound power to shape one's character, for good or ill. We may not choose to ban but we can and should condemn music that valorizes and delights in misogyny, racism, or gratuitous violence. At the extremes, such a view seems more like an obvious fact than reactionary raving.[37]

We find a similar story when we consider Kongzi's concern with proper attire. Many will find it at best quaint that he shuddered to think of what might happen to society if people began "folding their robes to the left instead of the right."[38] But in this case, too, the difference between Kongzi and what we might call the common-sense view in contemporary western society is one of degree and not kind. First, as was the case with music, one can have greater sympathy for Kongzi's position when he is arguing for the need to have proper attire in certain ritual contexts. Clearly, people feel more confidence in the legitimacy of standards of attire in cases such as funerals or weddings than when people are at leisure. But don't we also expect bankers to present us with a certain "look?" Don't we want them to appear as "solid" and "sensible" as the buildings they inhabit?[39] Don't we also draw certain conclusions about character based upon the attire of our companions on a first date?[40] The point is that attire can be a way to express certain attitudes and consciously expressing attitudes by wearing certain attire can contribute significantly to the formation of character.[41]

The practice of the rites and the reading of the *Odes* were both pursuits with a moral dimension, integral parts of the larger project of self cultivation. The person who successfully completed this process developed an enhanced sensitivity in understanding and explaining traditional patterns and applying them to actual affairs. Such a person could and would, on occasions when the situation warrants, depart from the traditional forms in order to realize the greater goal that these patterns were designed to achieve.[42] The practices of Confucian moral self cultivation were not designed to blindly *habituate* people to virtue, and though their full realization would, under normal circumstances, result in a variety of both material and psychological goods, they could not successfully be cultivated solely with the aim of acquiring such goods.

The pursuit ultimately must be as an *expression* of who one is, a follower of the Way.[43]

In addition to offering a fascinating program of moral learning, the practices, attitudes, and aspirations associated with Kongzi's *acquisition model* of self cultivation provided the foundation and set the direction of one of the longest-lived and richest traditions of moral self cultivation the world has produced.

# Notes

1. For an impressive anthology, representing a broad range of recent scholarship on Kongzi and his writings, see Bryan W. Van Norden, ed., *Confucius and the Analects: New Essays* (New York: Oxford University Press, 2000). For a dated though still helpful study of Kongzi and his thought, see Herrlee G. Creel, *Confucius: The Man and the Myth* (New York: John Day Co., 1949).

2. The primary source of information we have about Kongzi comes from the 論語 *Lunyu* "Analects," a record of his sayings and conversations and those of some of his students. The text contains material from a variety of different sources and times. I will not explore the textual issues here but have avoided using any passages that are clearly of dubious provenance. In my references to the text, I follow the numbering found in the Harvard-Yenching Institute's concordance to the *Analects*. English translations either follow or approximate this organization of the text. For a translation and study of the text that seeks to reconstruct Kongzi's original message, see Bruce E. and Taeko A. Brooks, *The Original Analects: Sayings of Confucius and His Successors* (New York: Columbia University Press, 1998).

3. Kongzi was and saw himself as a member of a group called the *ru* 儒 "Erudites" or "Learned," so it makes little sense to describe him as a "Confucian." However, it makes perfectly good sense to describe his later followers—who explicitly declare their allegiance to Kongzi and his way of life—as "Confucians." All of the remaining thinkers whose thought we will explore in this volume are Confucians in this sense.

4. *Analects* 7.1. The degree to which Kongzi innovated is an issue of considerable disagreement among contemporary scholars. In their recent book *Thinking Through Confucius* (Albany, NY: SUNY Press, 1987), Roger T. Ames and David L. Hall describe Kongzi as a flexible and fluid innovator. My view is somewhere between this and the caricature of an ossified ritualist often foisted upon Kongzi and his followers. For my view, see my review of *Thinking Through Confucius* in *Philosophy East and West*, 41.2, (April, 1991): 241-54 and my analysis of the Confucian golden rule in "Reweaving the 'one thread' of the *Analects*," *Philosophy East and West*, 40.1 (January, 1990): 17-33.

5. Applying the work of Jonathan Z. Smith in "The Influence of Symbols on Social Change: A Place to Stand," *Worship*, 44, (1970): 457-74, to the Confucian tradition, Lee H. Yearley describes it as a *locative religion*. See Yearley's "A Confucian Crisis: Mencius' Two Cosmogonies and Their Ethics," in Robin W. Lovin and Frank E. Reynolds, eds., *Cosmogony and Ethical Order: New Studies in Comparative Ethics* (Chicago: University of Chicago Press, 1985): 310-27.

6. The relationship between the rightness of the Way and its happy consequences is a tension that runs throughout the Confucian tradition (and many others as well). Confucians insist that one follows the Way because it is the Way and not for the benefits to be derived therefrom. At the same time, they insist, with equal conviction, that only the Way can lead to a harmonious and flourishing society. There is a tension, though not a contradiction, here. I discuss this issue briefly in *Ethics in the Confucian Tradition: The Thought of Mencius and Wang Yang-ming* (Atlanta: Scholars Press, 1990): 5-13 and in more detail in "Character Consequentialism: An Early Confucian Contribution to Contemporary Ethical Theory," *The Journal of Religious Ethics*, 19.1 (Spring, 1991): 55-70.

7. Confucius' sense of mission is an often overlooked and under appreciated aspect of his thought. But he clearly saw himself in such terms. Once, when his life was in danger in the state of Kuang, he said, "Since the death of [the sage] King Wen, has not [true] culture resided here within me? If Heaven wants to destroy this culture, then those who come after my death will be unable to encounter it. If Heaven does not want to destroy this culture, what can the men of Kuang do to me?" (*Analects* 9.5).

8. The only place in the *Analects* where Kongzi mentions the concept of *xing* 性 "human nature" is *Analects* 17.2, where he says, "By nature people are close to one another, by practice they are far apart." This, of course, is consistent with either Mengzi's or Xunzi's position or with any number of intermediary positions between these two extremes. The only other occurrence of the character *xing* in the *Analects* is 5.13, where a disciple, Zigong, tells us the master did not (or did not often) speak about this topic.

9. I explore this issue in considerable detail in "Thinking and Learning in Early Confucianism," *Journal of Chinese Philosophy*, 17 (1990): 473-93.

10. *Analects* 2.7. An example which illustrates that Kongzi's concern was with developing a kind of know-how is *Analects* 13.5, "One who can recite the three hundred *Odes* but when entrusted with an affair of government cannot carry it through, or commissioned as a representative to some distant land is unable to respond on the spot; though such a one knows much, what use is it?"

11. For example, see *Analects* 11.10 where Kongzi mourns excessively for his favorite disciple Yan Hui, or 13.18 where he insists that "upright" behavior is extremely context-sensitive. I discuss this general issue at some length in "Reweaving the 'one thread' of the *Analects*."

12. *Analects* 2.15. Notice that thinking in a vacuum is even worse than mere rote learning. It seems that, devoid of the context which tradition provides, one will not only not progress, one will go astray.

13. Arthur Waley is the first to notice this important distinction. See his discussion in *The Analects of Confucius* (New York: Vintage Books, 1938): 44-46.

14. In the thought of Mengzi, the notion of *si* comes to mean the mental act of focusing on one's moral intuitions. For a discussion of this aspect of Mengzi's thought, see Bryan W. Van Norden, "Mengzi and Xunzi: Two Views of Human Agency," in T. C. Kline III and Philip J. Ivanhoe, eds., *Virtue, Nature, and Moral Agency in the Xunzi* (Indianapolis, IN: Hackett Publishing Company, 2000).

15. For examples, see *Analects* 4.17, 14.12, 14.26, 16.10, and 19.1.

16. *Analects* 9.30. The lines quoted are from a poem not included in the present edition of the *Odes*. The *Shi* 詩 (*Odes, Book of Odes*, or *Book of Songs*) is a collection of rhymed poems derived from early folk songs and ceremonial incantations. Tradition claims that Kongzi edited an earlier group of three thousand poems down to three hundred, but modern scholars regard this as myth. Kongzi regarded the *Odes* as a repository of wisdom but one that required a sophisticated sensibility and deep reflection to properly understand.

17. This seems to be the sense of the character in *Analects* 2.15, 15.31, 19.6, and perhaps 5.20 as well.

18. The *Odes* also provided a source of general knowledge and useful common allusions for the educated person of the day. D. C. Lau discusses both these aspects of the *Odes* in the preface to his translation of the *Analects*. See *The Analects* (New York: Dorset Press, 1979): 41-2. Some scholars have claimed that Kongzi intentionally twisted the meaning of the *Odes* to fit the particular occasion. See for example, Waley, *Analects*, p. 89 note #1 and p. 90 note #3. For a more developed and nuanced statement of this position, see Steven Van Zoeren, *Poetry and Personality* (Stanford, CA: Stanford University Press, 1991).

19. *Analects* 2.2. I read this line according to the earliest extant commentary, as does D. C. Lau in his translation.

20. Zigong's personal name.

21. *Analects* 1.15. See 3.8 for another example of this kind of exchange.

22. For example, see *Analects* 2.2, 2.11, 4.15, etc.

23. A most insightful discussion of the role of ritual in Kongzi's thought and its modern relevance can be found in Herbert Fingarette, *Confucius—the Secular as Sacred* (New York: Harper and Row, 1972). For an insightful critique of Fingarette's more controversial claims, see Benjamin

I. Schwartz, *The World of Thought in Ancient China* (Cambridge, MA: The Belknap Press, 1985). See also the review of Fingarette by Henry Rosemont, Jr., in *Philosophy East and West*, 26.4 (October, 1976): 463-77 and the response and reply in *Philosophy East and West*, 28.4 (October, 1978): 511-14 and 515-19. In addition, see the review by Chad Hansen in *Journal of Chinese Philosophy*, 3 (1976): 197-204 and Fingarette's reply, *Journal of Chinese Philosophy*, 7 (1980): 259-66.

24. *Analects* 3.11. The rites were the outward manifestation, the embodiment of, the *Dao*, which provided the ultimate meaning of life for Kongzi. See *Analects* 4.8.

25. Here, I translate the Chinese character *ren* 仁 as "humanity" instead of the more often used "benevolence" since for Kongzi it has the sense of the most general virtue governing interpersonal relationships and human life. While benevolence is *part* of this ideal it is not a sufficiently comprehensive notion and tends to mislead.

26. *Analects* 12.1. Many western interpreters tend to focus on the latter part of this passage and thus read it as a rather mechanistic list of prohibitions. This makes the passage seem more like a secular version of the Ten Commandments. But the first part of the passage, together with what Kongzi says in other places in the text, emphasizes the need for one freely to *give oneself over* to the practice of ritual.

27. *Analects* 3.7. This example illustrates both the restraining function of ritual and its ability to simultaneously engender an attitude of humility. For another example, which employs notions of good sportsmanship in hunting and fishing, see 7.28. Arthur Waley was the first to recognize this aspect of Kongzi's thought. See Waley, *Analects*, p. 55. These passages provide excellent examples of an issue over which Confucian and Daoist thinkers disagree and diverge. The former see social interrelationships as challenging but integral to human flourishing; one must develop the self to be able to meet these challenges. The latter see society and its various demands as corrupt and corrupting. Compare the view of the *Daodejing*, chapter 5, "Hunting and riding make one's mind wild with excitement" or *Zhuangzi*, chapter 4, "When men get together to pit their strength in games of skill, they start off in a light and friendly mood, but usually end up in a dark and angry one . . . When men meet at some ceremony to drink, they start off in an orderly manner, but usually end up in disorder . . ." See Burton Watson, tr., *The Complete Works of Chuang Tzu* (New York: Columbia University Press, 1968): 60-1.

28. In regard to the first of these three moral failings, both a mechanical adherence to ritual or the idea that a certain behavior, for example, a particular form of greeting, is "mere etiquette" reflect a degraded conception of what such ritual was designed to encourage. At its worst, such attitudes can lead the obtuse performer to insist on certain conduct to the point of making a guest or new acquaintance uncomfortable or even severely embarrassed. This is to realize the exact opposite of what such rituals are intended to achieve.

Philippa Foot seems to imply something like this kind of disdain for "mere etiquette" in her otherwise insightful article, "Morality as a System of Hypothetical Imperatives," in *Virtues and Vices* (Berkeley, CA: University of California Press, 1978): 157-73. However, her position can be seen as providing support for the interpretation of ritual presented here. The "reason-giving force" of ritual is its contribution to a well-lived life.

Timidity and the difference between daring or machismo and the courage shown in standing up to a threat in order to realize a greater good provide good illustrations of actions that can parade as virtue but tend toward vice, the second of our three failings. And finally, in several passages in the *Analects*, we find Kongzi deeply concerned about his disciples becoming what I have elsewhere called "moral martinets." See my "Reweaving the 'one thread' of the *Analects*."

One might also see, in this passage, the kernel of Xunzi's later objection to Mengzi's theory that human nature is good. Kongzi seems to be saying that any tendency we have—even good ones like caring—are not really moral until they are ethicized through the rites. Xunzi insists that until a desire or inclination is transformed through ritual it is not only not good, it tends toward the bad. For the definitive work describing this aspect of Xunzi's thought, see Eric L. Hutton, "Does Xunzi Have a Consistent Theory of Human Nature?" in Kline and Ivanhoe, *Virtue, Nature, and Moral Agency in the Xunzi.*

29. *Analects* 8.2. Cf. 17.8.

30. *Analects* 10.12.

31. *Analects* 7.4, 10.5.

32. For an insightful review of the best and most influential contemporary interpretations of Kongzi's conception of ritual, along with a sensitive, powerful, and new interpretation of its significance, see Stephen H. Wilson, "Conformity, Individuality, and the Nature of Virtue," in Van Norden, *Confucius and the Analects.*

33. *Analects* 7.9. See also 9.10.

34. In regard to human character, Kongzi had a very broad conception of the good. In contrast, contemporary western accounts of virtue and character—unlike for example Aristotle's— tend to focus on a narrow range of clearly moral traits. For an insightful and wise exception to this trend, see Joel J. Kupperman, *Character* (New York: Oxford University Press, 1991).

35. Music, for Kongzi, meant primarily the music and accompanying dances performed at court. Here he was particularly concerned with the effects such performances had upon the ruling elite. However, his point would seem to have equal force in more general application. Kongzi himself played the lute (*Analects* 17.20) and whenever he heard someone sing a song that he liked, he would wait until they had finished, ask them to repeat it, and sing along in harmony with them (*Analects* 7.32). For an interesting study of the

roles music can play in the good human life, see Kathleen Higgins, *The Music of Our Lives* (Philadelphia, PA: Temple University Press, 1991). For an article that focuses on the role of music in the Confucian tradition, see her "Music in Confucian and Neo-Confucian Philosophy," *International Philosophical Quarterly*, 20.4 (December, 1980): 433-51.

36. *Analects* 15.10. See 8.8 for music's contribution to self cultivation. For Kongzi's praise of the *Shao*, see 7.14. See 3.25 where he compares this with martial music that is "perfectly good but not perfectly beautiful." Finally, see 3.23 for music as a general metaphor for measured and harmonious action.

37. It is illuminating to note both the similarities and differences between Kongzi's view of music and that proffered by Plato in the *Republic*. For both, music plays an important role in the formation of character. But for Plato it is part of the general "musical" education that the young must undergo if they are to be molded into virtuous individuals. Music makes the *young* soul receptive to order and reason so that dialectic can then work effectively upon it. For Plato, such an education is the only way to bring the recalcitrant passionate nature into accord with reasoned judgments. For Kongzi, the reshaping of the self is accomplished largely through ritual practice and internalization of the lessons contained in the *Odes*. Dialectic plays no central role in this process and the young need not first be tamed by music. Music is very important for Kongzi, and equally important at the final stages of self cultivation. For a discussion of Plato's views see Gregory Vlastos, *Socrates: Ironist and Moral Philosopher* (Ithaca, NY: Cornell University Press, 1991): 88-9.

38. *Analects* 14.17. For other examples dealing with attire, see 10.6, 10.19.

39. Metaphors like "solid" and "sensible" move easily across both people and certain institutions. Both embody particular qualities and each can invoke the feelings (in this case security and trust) that are commonly associated with these qualities. For a revealing analysis of how metaphors operate in these ways, see Kendall L. Walton, "Projectivism, Empathy and Musical Tension" in *Philosophical Topics* (Forthcoming).

40. I am not arguing that there is some absolute "dress code" to which people must all adhere, only that we often make judgments about how much a person *cares* by how much attention they devote to their personal appearance, particularly on special occasions. Such judgments are neither irrational nor unwarranted. Moreover, they presuppose some shared sense of what is appropriate for a given occasion; they make sense only in a *social* setting.

41. For an at times amusing, at times disturbing, analysis of attire as an indicator of social class in American society, see Paul Fussell, *Class* (New York: Ballantine Books, 1983).

42. This aspect of the role of moral education and the relationship between received rules and developed intuitions is most evident in Kongzi's form of the golden rule. For a study of this aspect of Kongzi's thought, see my "Reweaving the 'one thread' of the *Analects*."

43. In this regard pursuing them represents an *expressive* rather than an *acquisitive* desire. For this distinction, see Terence Irwin, *Plato's Moral Theory: The Early and Middle Dialogues* (Oxford: Clarendon Press, 1977): 239-41. The ideal for Kongzi was to embody the virtues so thoroughly that their performance flowed forth spontaneously. For an insightful exploration of the role of spontaneity in Kongzi's philosophy, see Joel Kupperman, "Naturalness Revisited: Why Western Philosophers Should Read Confucius" in Van Norden, *Confucius and the Analects*.

# 孟子

# 2. Mengzi ("Mencius")

Kongzi's proposals, about the proper shape and meaning of human life, and the path one must travel to get there, soon generated widespread and intense debate. A variety of different thinkers came forward to propose alternative pictures of how society should be organized and how people should live their lives. Kongzi's passing marked the beginning of a three- to four-hundred-year period profoundly rich in social, ethical, political, and religious thought. In terms of the variety of views presented, it is arguably without parallel in human history.[1] Prominent among the opponents to Kongzi's vision were two groups: the followers of Mozi (the *Mohists*); and the followers of Yang Zhu.

The Mohists[2] objected to many aspects of the Confucian vision, but perhaps most importantly, they argued against the Confucian claim that our moral sense must develop in relation to and remain partial to our immediate family members. In direct opposition to this central Confucian claim, the Mohists argued that we should show equal and impartial care for all people.[3]

Mozi and his followers had a rather thin picture of human nature and as a result a relatively simple view of moral psychology.[4] Not unlike Socrates, they believed that people were highly rational creatures, and that a well-turned argument would have an inexorable pull on any person who could follow its course. As a consequence of this aspect of their views, they paid a great deal of attention to the form and method of argumentation, resulting in considerable advances in logic, mathematics, and optics, among other disciplines.[5] The Mohists also shared the widely held belief that people would respond in kind to the treatment they received and that most people had an innate tendency to defer to and try to please their superiors. For those who would not respond in any of these ways, the Mohists made an additional, more coercive, appeal to the role that ghosts and spirits play in maintaining justice in the world. Given these various views about human nature and ethical motivation, the Mohists were led to condemn Confucian ritual and cultural practices, such as music, as pointless and extravagant.

The Mohists are best described as materialist, state consequentialists. Like other consequentialists, one of the great strengths of their position is the clear criteria they offer for what is right and good. According to the Mohists, one should act in a way that maximizes the greatest amount of overall, material good for the state, with the good described in terms of the wealth, order, and population of the state.[6] Together with their call for impartial caring, Mohist consequentialism offered an appealing and powerful alternative to Kongzi's traditional

15

vision. With their superior rhetorical abilities, the Mohists proved to be formidable opponents to later Confucians and seemed to have enjoyed considerable success.[7] And they were not alone.

Yang Zhu and his followers offered another, appealing alternative.[8] According to Yang Zhu, both the Mohists and Confucians were wrong. He seems to have believed that the Mohists had too impoverished a picture of what human beings were like; nobody, or at least very few people, could live as they suggested. More important, no one would choose to live as Mozi urged, if adequately apprised of proper alternatives and afforded the opportunity to pursue them. According to Yang Zhu, the Mohist life was contrary to human nature, and therefore, it could not be sustained. The Confucians, too, were wrong. They had a more robust picture of human nature, but it was the wrong picture. They over-embellished and thereby distorted the natural simplicity of our nature by following a set of traditional ritual practices. Rather than completing human nature, these practices twisted and deformed it. Kongzi and his followers offered no explicit arguments for why one should follow tradition, only the promise that by doing so everything would work out for the best. In response, Yang Zhu argued that the proper goal of human life was to be as Heaven made us: to be *natural*. The true character of human nature was to provide and care for oneself and to live out one's years. Yang Zhu was a special kind of egoist, one who didn't see social participation as, in any significant degree, integral to personal satisfaction or human flourishing.[9]

At this point in history, Mengzi (391-308 B.C.E.) emerged to take up the defense of the Confucian cause.[10] His particular statement of the Confucian vision took form, to a significant extent, as a response to the Mohist and Yangist challenges. On several occasions, Mengzi expresses his alarm concerning how popular the ideas of Mozi and Yang Zhu had become, and in one revealing passage, he gives us some idea of what he thought of the followers of these two thinkers and their relationship to Confucianism.

> Those who desert the Mohist School are sure to turn to Yang Zhu and those who desert the Yangist School are sure to turn to us. When they come to us, we simply accept them. Nowadays, those who debate the followers of Yang and Mo act as though they were chasing runaway pigs. Even after they get them back in the pen, they go and tie up their legs.[11]

This passage makes at least two important points. The latter part is an admonition, perhaps directed at some of Mengzi's own disciples, concerning the error of castigating recent converts to the Confucian cause. Its point seems to be connected to the first part of the passage, where

Mengzi describes a natural progression of understanding and allegiance, leading from Mo to Yang and then to Kongzi. The thought here seems to be that people can and must find their own way to the truth. One cannot deny other people their autonomy without perhaps fatally undermining the course of their progress.

But why might Mengzi believe in the "natural" progression described in this passage and what is the nature of this course of development? Perhaps he believed that most of those who try to follow the Mohist way will find it asks too much of them. People in general just cannot be impartial about whom they care for to the degree the Mohists insist upon. Most find that they cannot ignore the deep and persistent urgings of their nature—as Mengzi understood it—and this will lead them to forget the state in favor of their kin, friends, and acquaintances.[12] People who try the Mohist way and find that it does not sustain them, will abandon this overly idealist and other-directed life and turn instead to their own more local concerns, and so it is "natural" that they will turn to Yang Zhu's way. But Mengzi is confident that when they seek for satisfaction by following Yang Zhu, they will again be disappointed. For one cannot find true and complete satisfaction in life by aiming at it directly, seeking *only* for one's own satisfaction and local concerns. Part of what we seek comes from living a life that is not only good for particular individuals but one that is good for humans in general. And since by nature we are social creatures, the good life for us must accommodate the social and political dimensions of life. But those who have turned away from Mozi and to Yang Zhu are looking in the right place, they are looking within themselves and not to some *exterior* doctrine, as do the Mohists. And so Mengzi believes that they will discover the truth of Confucianism; that, as human beings, they can find meaning and satisfaction in life only by becoming *moral people*. It turns out that fulfilling familial and social obligations not only is not in conflict with personal satisfaction, these obligations lie at the very center of the good life. With this realization, these people will join the Confucian fold.

Mengzi explicitly linked the task of self cultivation with the development of one's Heavenly conferred nature; he maintained the structure of Kongzi's original vision, but set it upon a new foundation, a subtle yet powerful theory about human nature.[13] One can see Mengzi's philosophical views as part of an emerging debate about the true character of human nature. Mengzi believed that, by nature, human beings are inclined toward the good, and that if we reflect upon and accord with this inclination, we will develop into full moral beings and fulfill the grand Confucian vision. Like many early Chinese thinkers, he believed that to *develop* oneself according to one's true nature is to fulfill a design inscribed by Heaven upon our human hearts. To follow the natural, then, is to obey Heaven, and to develop oneself is to serve Heaven.[14] Given such assumptions, the central ethical question then becomes: What *constitutes* following one's nature?

Mengzi begins to answer this question by arguing that we are born with a nascent moral sense. To be precise, he believes we have four nascent moral senses: for benevolence, righteousness, propriety, and right and wrong.[15] He refers to these nascent moral dispositions as *duan* 端 "sprouts," and his choice of metaphor is critical to what he seeks to convey.[16] For like sprouts, our moral sense is a *visible and active*, not *hidden or latent*, part of the self.[17] Mengzi has a variety of different arguments to establish the existence of the moral sprouts, but I will discuss only two: his arguments based on *give-away actions* and those based on *thought experiments*.[18]

The notion of a give-away action is used in the philosophical analysis of self-deception. People who are self-deceived must both in some sense know something is the case and yet hide this knowledge from themselves and deny that this is so. For example, a young man might deny that he loves a young woman and yet *in some deep sense* he knows that he loves her. Other people who observe his behavior know that he loves her—despite his repeated denials—because they see him engage in a variety of activities that can only be understood as being motivated by such love. For example, he *just happens* to keep a record of every occasion he has met her, he *just happens* to maintain lists of her preferences and close friends, he *just happens* to walk—far out of his way—to pass by her window as he returns from work each day and he regularly talks about getting a tatoo of her name inscribed within the borders of a burning heart. All these actions *give-away* his true feelings, and with any luck, his friends will help him realize his love for her by pointing these things out.

Mengzi relies upon such give-away actions in his moral teaching. He points out instances where a person unknowingly has acted in a moral way, where the only plausible explanation for so acting is that this individual was motivated by some innate altruistic desire. For example, in a conversation with King Xuan of Qi, Mengzi recounts an occasion when the king spared an ox that he happened to see as it was being led to slaughter.[19] Taking pity on the ox, because of its frightened appearance and mournful cries, the king had it freed and replaced with a sheep. By questioning the king carefully, Mengzi leads him to see that the "heart" manifested in this act is the "sprout" of benevolence. The king spontaneously understood and manifested not merely an awareness of the ox's suffering but a concern for its well-being. His conversation with Mengzi moves the king to quote and comment on the *Odes*:

The king was pleased and said, "The *Odes* says, 'The heart belongs to another. But through reflection, I take its measure.' This describes you perfectly! For though I did the deed, when I turned to search within myself, I could not understand my own feelings. But when you described these events, it stirred my heart."[20]

Mengzi also employs "thought-experiments" to argue for the existence of the moral sprouts. By this I mean he invokes hypothetical scenarios and then asks us to imagine what would occur were such conditions to obtain. Albert Einstein employed such thought-experiments to great effect in theoretical physics, asking us to imagine what would happen to time and space if one were on a spacecraft traveling at the speed of light. Unlike such an imaginative excursion—which is in principle impossible to actually experience—Mengzi's moral thought-experiments describe quite ordinary experiences that offer a compelling case for the existence of a nascent, innate moral sense.

For example, he asks us to imagine the case of a person who suddenly and without warning sees a child about to fall into a well.[21] He asks, would not such a person immediately experience a feeling of alarm and concern for the child?[22] And would this feeling not be motivated purely out of one's innate disposition to feel sympathetic concern for an innocent human being? A fascinating aspect to such moral thought experiments is that if Mengzi is right, all of us, in contemplating this hypothetical scenario and reflecting upon it, will imaginatively experience *our own* moral sprouts. That is to say, we too will feel a "stirring in our hearts" that testifies to our own standing disposition to feel sympathetic concern for our fellow human beings. Mengzi will have gotten us to take the first step in our own moral self cultivation.

At this point, Mengzi's claim is quite modest: at most he has shown that we have *some* moral sensitivity as part of our nature. This won't get us very far. One might admit that such a sense exists and still maintain that it is such a weak motivation for action that it rarely, if ever, determines or guides one's conduct. Even if we accept Mengzi's belief that one should follow one's nature, the mere existence of the sprouts won't lead us to become moral.

Mengzi develops his case by going on to argue that there is a *natural structure* to the self and each part of us has a *natural function* to fulfill.[23] Of critical importance is the role that our *xin* 心 "heart" plays. For the early Chinese the *xin* contained cognitive (i.e., rational) faculties, affective (i.e., emotional) faculties—including the four moral "sprouts"—as well as volitional abilities (something akin to but distinct from our common notion of will), so it is best thought of as the "heart and mind."[24] Mengzi argued that unlike our other parts, our *xin* is able to consider, weigh, and judge between competing courses of action. Because the *xin* and only the *xin* performs this function, it is the natural governor of the self. And since, in order to fulfill Heaven's grand design for us and for the world, we must exercise each of our parts according to its individual natural function, we must think and reflect about the things we do. If we do this, we bring into play our innate moral sense.

> Gongduzi said, "All are equally human. Why is it that some become great and others small?"
> Mengzi replied, "Those who follow what is great within them become great; those who follow what is small become small."
> Gongduzi then said, "All are equally human. Why is it that some follow what is great and others follow what is small?"
> Mengzi replied, "It is not the function of the ear or the eye to reflect, and so they can become obsessed with things. Being unreflective, when they come in contact with other things, they are led astray. The function of the mind is to reflect. When it reflects, it gets things right; if it does not reflect, it cannot get things right. These are what Heaven has given us. If one takes one's stand in the great that is within, the small cannot take it away. This is what makes one great."[25]

Mengzi needs only one further claim to make a plausible case and this concerns the joy of moral action. He argues that if we monitor and assess our reactions to the things we think and do by an internal act of *si* "reflection" or "concentration," we will be guided toward good actions and away from bad.[26] The contemplation of good acts produces a special feeling of joy in us which in turn reinforces the moral sense and enables us, through a process of *extension*,[27] to do more and more difficult actions.[28] In Mengzi's own terms, such joy nourishes the moral sprouts; it provides them with a special kind of *qi* 氣 "energy." Mengzi called this special energy the *haoran zhi qi* 浩然之氣 "flood-like energy";[29] it is the energy of moral courage, the motivation or power that enables one to perform difficult moral tasks. Like the energy of any living thing, the moral sprouts thrive when properly nourished, and without such nourishment, they wither away.[30]

Mengzi uses a variety of agricultural metaphors to express his view of how the moral sprouts are to be cultivated. These metaphors reveal significant aspects of his ethical theory and, in particular, his views on moral self cultivation.[31] Let us focus upon two aspects of these agricultural metaphors: first, the gradual nature of this process, and second, the need for it to occur within a certain kind of environment.

Mengzi warns us not to rush the process of moral self cultivation in the parable of the Farmer of Song. The parable, in part, goes like this:

> There was a man of Song who pulled at his shoots of grain, because he was anxious for them to grow. After pulling on the shoots, he went home, not realizing what he had done. He said to his family, "I am worn out today; I have been helping the grain to grow." His son rushed out of the house to look at their plants and found that they all had withered.[32]

Mengzi goes on to say that one "must neither neglect one's shoots nor force them to grow." The former course of action will result in a lack of progress, but the latter will do positive harm. What then is one supposed to do? It seems that while the task of moral self cultivation requires one to be attentive to and actively involved in the process, one must not rush the course of one's moral development and attempt to do things that one is not quite ready to do. Mengzi has in mind here the person who wants to be a better person but doesn't want to face the fact that moral development is a long and difficult process that depends more on a steady accumulation of simple acts than a grand display of goodness. If, in the initial stages of moral development, one forsakes the simple acts and attempts something of grand proportion, even if one succeeds in doing the grand deed, the likelihood is that one will on some level *regret* doing it.[33] This can cause one to come to resent the entire process of moral self cultivation and lead one, mistakenly, to conclude that one just isn't up to the task. Unless one has a lively and wholehearted involvement in the moral acts one performs, unless one can, on some level, *feel* that one should act in this way, they will not only fail to help, they may actually hinder one's effort.[34] Like love, moral improvement "don't come easy." It requires the cultivation of knowledge, sensitivities, and dispositions that are won only through patient and prolonged application. The desire to be a good person can itself pose an impediment to moral improvement, if it encourages one to work beyond one's moral means. Improper moral cultivation causes one's moral sprouts to wither rather than flourish.

The final point concerns Mengzi's claim that for most people, the process of moral self cultivation must take place within a certain kind of environment. Though there are rare moral heroes who are able to successfully pursue the task of moral self cultivation even in the harshest of environments,[35] most of us need certain minimal conditions if we are to have a reasonable chance of success.

> Mengzi said, "In years of plenty, many young people are reliable, but in years of want many cannot control themselves. It is not because of their Heavenly conferred endowments that such

differences exist. It is because of what their hearts become mired in."³⁶

An environment devoid of basic necessities and comforts, good examples, and proper encouragement will usually prove impossible to overcome. Under such unhealthy conditions, most people will fail to develop their natural moral sensibilities. Their moral sprouts will become stunted and, overgrown with less noble tendencies, they may even become difficult to discern.

Even the best of moral teachers may be unable to help someone first embarking on the task of self cultivation overcome a harsh environment. Mengzi describes his own failure to help King Xuan of Qi:

> Do not be puzzled by the king's lack of wisdom. Even the most easily grown thing in all the world will not grow if it is given only one day of warmth for every ten days of cold. I see the king only rarely and when I withdraw, those whose effect upon him is like the cold arrive at his side. Though I draw forth some *meng* 萌 "sprouts" what good does it do?³⁷

The process of development which Mengzi describes, at least for most people, must take place within the context of a certain kind of human society. The moral sprouts we have are innate, but they require both conscious and concerted effort and a proper environment in order to develop as they should. Here we see the integral relationship between Confucian ethical philosophy and their political and social theory. Confucians believe that one cannot successfully pursue the ethical life outside of fulfilling certain familial and social obligations. One cannot develop a moral sense without knowing what it is to love and be loved within a human family,³⁸ and one cannot love and care for one's family without a deep and abiding concern for the society in which one lives.

One might think of Mengzi's claims about the innate good tendencies of human nature and their development into full moral dispositions using the analogy of human language. Our moral sprouts are innate, it is our nature to develop them, and this process requires a certain kind of environment. In the same way, human beings have an innate ability to speak human language, but this innate ability must be developed, and this requires a certain kind of benign environment.³⁹ Specifically, it requires caring family members and a community of fellow conversationalists. In both cases, too, a good deal of persistent individual effort must be applied if one is to realize fully the extraordinary nature of this innate inclination. In order to realize Heaven's design and become fully human, one must work to *develop* one's nature, and this development requires one to participate fully in familial and social life.

*Notes*

1. This state of affairs is accurately reflected in the title and substance of Benjamin I. Schwartz's revealing study of the period, *The World of Thought in Ancient China*. Other indispensible studies of this period include: A. C. Graham's *Disputers of the Tao* (LaSalle, IN: Open Court Press, 1989) and the more traditional, though less analytical, Wing-tsit Chan, *A Source Book in Chinese Philosophy* (Princeton, NJ: Princeton University Press, 1963) and Fung Yu-lan, *A History of Chinese Philosophy*, Derk Bodde, tr. (Princeton, NJ: Princeton University Press, 1953).

2. For a study of Mozi's philosophy, see Y. P. Mei, *Mo-tse, the Neglected Rival of Confucius* (London: Arthur Probsthain, 1934) and Philip J. Ivanhoe, "Mohist Philosophy" in *The Routledge Encyclopedia of Philosophy*, vol. 6 (London: Routledge Press, 1998): 451-55. For a study of the religious dimensions of Mozi's thought, see Scott Lowe, *Mo Tzu's Religious Blueprint for a Chinese Utopia* (Lewiston, ME: Edwin Mellon Press, Ltd., 1992). For a remarkable study of later Mohist thought, see A. C. Graham, *Later Mohist Logic, Ethics and Science* (Hong Kong: The Chinese University Press, 1978).

3. For a fascinating essay which argues for the reconciliation of these opposing perspectives, see David B. Wong, "Universalism versus Love with Distinctions: An Ancient Debate Revived," *Journal of Chinese Philosophy* 16:3-4 (September-December, 1989): 251-72.

4. Mozi appears to have been strongly voluntaristic, though some of his later followers, e.g., Yi Zhi, seem to have softened his voluntarism. See David S. Nivison, "Two Roots or One?" *Proceedings and Addresses of the American Philosophical Association*, 53.6 (August, 1980): 739-61. For an interesting alternative reading of Yi Zhi's position, see Kwong-loi Shun, "Mencius' Criticism of Mohism: An Analysis of *Meng Tzu* 3A:5," *Philosophy East and West*, 41.2 (April, 1991): 203-14.

5. The most thorough study of these aspects of later Mohist thought is Graham, *Later Mohist Logic*. Also of great interest is Joseph Needham, *Science and Civilization in China*, vol. 2 (Cambridge: Cambridge University Press, 1956): 168-84.

6. This is what Mozi describes as the task of "the benevolent man planning for the welfare of the world." See Burton Watson, tr., *Mo Tzu: Basic Writings* (New York: Columbia University Press, 1963): 65. See also the "Honoring the Worthy" chapter, p. 18. Mozi does seem to recognize honor as a psychological good, but it is not a central concern in his ethical theory. See Watson, pp. 18-33.

7. The Mohist school died out toward the end of the Warring States period perhaps because they were an organized, paramilitary group. Such a group would pose a considerable threat to the increasingly unified empire that eventually culminated in the Qin dynasty.

8. The most complete and incisive study of Yang Zhu and his thought is to be found in Graham, *Disputers*, pp. 53-64. Robert Eno questions Graham's views. For a summation of his objections, see his *The Confucian Creation of Heaven* (Albany: SUNY Press, 1990): 257-8, n. 41.

9. He was not, as he is often depicted, a hedonist. A life of hedonistic indulgence would surely prove injurious to "living out one's years," which was one of Yang Zhu's central goals. As Graham points out, it is also inaccurate and unfair to describe Yang Zhu (as Mengzi does) as fundamentally *selfish*. The good life for Yang Zhu included care of kin and friends. Moreover, he believed that each person tending to these more local, personal concerns, yielded the best overall results for everyone.

10. The dates for Mengzi's life are from David S. Nivison, "Meng Tzu," Mircea Eliade, ed., *The Encyclopedia of Religion*, vol. 9 (New York: MacMillan Book Company, 1987): 373-6.

11. *Mengzi*, 7B26. See also 3B9 and 7A26, etc.

12. A similar objection to Mohism is made in chapter 33 of the *Zhuangzi*. See Burton Watson, tr., *The Complete Works of Chuang Tzu* (New York: Columbia University Press, 1968): 364-7.

13. The two most important studies of Mengzi's theory of human nature are A. C. Graham, "The Background of the Mencian Theory of Human Nature," reprinted in his *Studies in Chinese Philosophy and Philosophical Literature* (Albany, NY: SUNY Press, 1990): 7-66, and D. C. Lau, "Theories of Human Nature in Mengzi and Xunzi" reprinted in T. C. Kline, and Philip J. Ivanhoe, *Virtue, Nature, and Moral Agency in the Xunzi*. Several important essays on Mengzi's philosophy can be found in David S. Nivison, *The Ways of Confucianism* (Chicago: Open Court Press, 1996). Advanced students will want to study Kwong-loi Shun's important work, *Mencius and Early Chinese Thought* (Stanford, CA: Stanford University Press, 1997) which offers an impressive survey and discussion of the secondary literature on many passages and problems in the text. My own understanding of Mengzi's theory of human nature and how it relates to his ethical teachings can be found in my *Ethics in the Confucian Tradition: The Thought of Mencius and Wang Yang-ming*.

14. See *Mengzi* 7A1. It is important to note that for Mengzi this meant attending to and according with certain spontaneous tendencies, exercising one's natural capacities for inquiry, reflection, and action and taking one's place in a grand cosmological scheme. It was *not* merely obeying the commands or according with the will of some deity or deities.

15. *Mengzi* 2A6 and 6A6. Another way of understanding Mengzi is to see him as holding that there is one moral sense that gets manifested in four different basic modes. Liu Xiusheng makes a very good case for something like this latter view, arguing that a general sense of benevolence or sympathetic concern is fundamental to the other "sprouts." This is not only philosophically interesting—making Mengzi's view similar in important

ways to thinkers like Hume—but also textually appealing, for Mengzi makes an explicit argument only for the heart of benevolence. See Liu Xiusheng, *The Place of Humanity in Ethics: Combined Insights from Hume and Mencius*, PhD Dissertation, Department of Philosophy, The University of Texas at Austin (December, 1999). For the notion of "sympathetic concern," see Stephen Darwall, "Empathy, Sympathy, Care," *Philosophical Studies*, 89 (1998): 261-82.

16. Mengzi uses the word *duan* repeatedly in 2A6, where he presents the clearest statement of this aspect of his view of human nature. He also uses other characters, for example *meng* 萌 "sprouts" and *nie* 蘖 "buds" in order to make related points about the growth and fragility of the moral sense in 6A8 and 6A9. In 2A2, we find the story of the Farmer of Song who pulls on his *miao* 苗 "spouts of grain" in a misguided effort to help them grow.

Translating *duan* as "sprout" reveals an extensive and complex metaphor that reappears throughout the text in different forms; for Mengzi, agriculture is a paradigm for self cultivation. D. C. Lau clearly understood that *duan* meant "sprout." See p. 214, n. #19 in the reprint of his early seminal work, "Mengzi and Xunzi on Human Nature." In her recent book, Sarah Allan discusses this issue with insight. See her *The Way of Water and Sprouts of Virtue* (Albany, NY: SUNY Press, 1997): 113-4.

17. In order for Mengzi's program of self cultivation to work, it must be the case that people *already* possess some active and visible moral capacity that they can attend to and develop. This feature of his view of human nature is critical for the two types of arguments he provides for the existence of the moral sprouts which we will examine here.

18. For a more complete discussion see my *Ethics in the Confucian Tradition: The Thought of Mencius and Wang Yang-ming*, pp. 73-9.

19. *Mengzi* 1A7.

20. *Mengzi* 1A7.

21. *Mengzi* 2A6.

22. Mengzi is not concerned here with the question of what such a person would *actually do* so much as what she would perceive and *experience*. To understand this example as saying that anyone in such a situation would rush over and *try to save* the child goes considerably beyond what the text describes; it only says a person in such a scenario will experience a "feeling of alarm and concern."

23. He argues for the first claim in *Mengzi* 6A14 and the second in 6A15. Also, in 7A1, we see that fully developing one's *xin* is the way to understand one's nature, which in turn is the way to understand Heaven.

24. See the entry for *hsin* (i.e., *xin*) by David S. Nivison in Mircea Eliade, eds., *The Encyclopedia of Religion*, vol. 6, pp. 477-8. Mengzi does not do an adequate job of sorting out the various aspects of the *xin* and is unclear about

important aspects of his moral psychology, e.g., the extent to which the mind can be affected by or contains bad inclinations as well as good. His view of volition is roughly that we possess the ability to steer and focus our attention on different parts of the heart and mind, thereby engaging (or disengaging) different emotional and intentional resources within the self.

25. *Mengzi* 6A15.

26. As I mentioned earlier (see pp. 2-3) in my discussion of Kongzi's method of self cultivation, Mengzi's sense of the character *si* marks a new development in its use as a term of art in moral psychology.

27. The western philosophical study of Mengzi's notion of moral extension began with David S. Nivison's seminal article, "Mencius and Motivation," in Henry Rosemont, Jr., ed., *Journal of the American Academy of Religion, Thematic Issue S* 47.3 (September, 1980): 417-32. His position at that time is developed by Kwong-loi Shun in "Moral Reasons in Confucian Ethics," *The Journal of Chinese Philosophy*, vol. 16 (1989): 317-43. Shun's view is discussed and criticized by Bryan W. Van Norden's subsequent essay, "Kwong-loi Shun on Moral Reasons in Mencius," *The Journal of Chinese Philosophy*, vol. 18 (1991): 353-70. The discussion continues in David B. Wong, "Is There a Distinction between Reason and Emotion in Mencius?" *Philosophy East and West*, 41.1 (January, 1991): 31-44 and Craig K. Ihara, "David Wong on Emotions in Mencius" *Philosophy East and West* 41.1 (January, 1991): 45-53. More recently, Nivison returned to this issue in a significantly revised and expanded article, "Motivation and Moral Action in Mencius" in *The Ways of Confucianism*, pp. 91-119. My analysis can be found in "Chinese Self Cultivation and Mencian Extension," *Journal of the History of Ideas* (Forthcoming).

28. See *Mengzi* 4A27. Contemplation of proposed courses of actions or the actions of others can enable us to perform more and more difficult moral acts by helping us to attain proper understanding and sensitivity. But Mengzi appears to believe that the motivation to perform more challenging moral actions comes only or at least primarily through reflection on moral actions that we actually have done.

29. See Mengzi 2A2 for a fascinating discussion of varieties of courage and the cultivation of the flood-like *qi*. For discussions of this topic in Mengzi's thought, see Lee H. Yearley, *Mencius and Aquinas: Theories of Virtue and Conceptions of Courage* (Albany, NY: SUNY Press, 1990) and Bryan W. Van Norden, "Mencius on Courage" in Peter A. French, Theodore E. Uehling, and Howard K. Wettstein, eds., *Midwest Studies in Philosophy*, vol. 21 (Notre Dame, IN: University of Notre Dame Press, 1997): 237-56. The most complete treatment of this topic can be found in Jiang Xinyan, *Courage, Passion and Virtue*, PhD Dissertation, Department of Philosophy, University of Cincinnati (1994).

30. Consider the following lines from 6A8, "And so all things will flourish if only they receive their proper nourishment and all will perish if

they do not." Here we see yet another example of agriculture as the paradigm for self cultivation. The idea is picked up and further developed in 6A9.

31. For example, see *Mengzi* 2A2, 2A6, 6A7, 6A8, 6A9, 6A19, etc.

32. *Mengzi* 2A2.

33. Consider *Mengzi* 7B11, "One who is fond of a good name may relinquish a state of a thousand chariots, but if one is not *really* this kind of person, giving away a cup of rice or a bowl of soup will show in one's face."

34. One might well be concerned that this view of things could lead one to continually put off difficult moral acts for another day. But, first, Mengzi believed that everyone had plenty of opportunities to perform helpful moral acts and therefore would *grow into* more difficult challenges, and, second, he does have his voluntarist moments in which he simply counsels procrastinating individuals to *just do it!* See for example, *Mengzi* 3B8. Mengzi's insistence that one be properly committed to the moral act does not mean that such individuals never experience the difficulty that often is involved in doing the right thing. They may often feel conflicting emotions. What Mengzi is saying is that they *must* feel the moral motivation to act in order for such actions to help in their moral development.

35. The most dramatic example of this is perhaps the sage emperor Shun, who overcame an abusive family situation to become the epitome of filial virtue. His good conduct eventually converted his father (see *Mengzi* 4A28, cf. 7A16). One also sees it in the person of Yi Yin and Mengzi's teaching that Heaven chooses certain individuals to "awaken first" (see *Mengzi* 5A7). In 6B15, he recalls the difficulties overcome by a number of sages and claims that Heaven places such challenges in the path of those it has chosen in order to steel them for the task ahead. And while Mengzi claims that all people are the same in kind as these sages, he also insists that *they* had a natural talent for morality. Mengzi says, "Yao and Shun had it as their nature. Tang and Wu embodied it. The five lord protectors borrowed from it. . . ." *Mengzi* 7A30, cf. 7B33. Since our moral sense is a natural capacity, Mengzi assumed that some people would prove to be naturally "gifted" in these ways.

36. *Mengzi* 6A7.

37. *Mengzi* 6A9.

38. Cf. *Mengzi* 7A15.

39. Cf. *Mengzi* 3B6. In a recent and fascinating work, Steven Pinker describes human beings as possessing a "language instinct." See Steven Pinker, *The Language Instinct* reprint (New York: HarperCollins Publishers, 1995). While this dramatic way of stating things is helpful in emphasizing the innate tendency we possess to acquire and use language, it can also mislead. For unlike other instincts, our ability to acquire and use language requires an inherited culture and other properly disposed—i.e., helpful and encouraging—language users. Feral children do not spontaneously become proficient language users, and if a child's ability to acquire language is not

developed early in life, it can never become proficient. If the same holds true for moral development, this would provide good warrants for focusing much more attention on early development, the vast majority of which occurs within the family.

# 荀子

# 3. Xunzi

We have explored how, on Mengzi's view of moral self cultivation, one begins with a nascent moral sense and through a process of reflection, study, and effort one gradually strengthens and extends this sense until it becomes a powerful and discriminating moral disposition. Mengzi uses a variety of agricultural metaphors to describe this *development model* of moral self cultivation, and the images he invokes capture the complex and dynamic interplay of environment, attention, effort, natural tendency, and what is probably best described as moral luck,[1] which he sees as defining the task of moral self cultivation. Mengzi believed that the development he described followed a natural process that would unfold when each part of the self was exercised in its proper role, according to its natural function. The *xin* "heart/mind" played a critically important role in this process, being that part of the self uniquely capable of entertaining, weighing, and choosing courses of actions. If exercised in its proper "office" of *si* "reflection," it will guide the self away from bad actions and toward the good. The fact that human beings are, in this way, innately inclined toward the good is the essential force of Mengzi's claim that *xingshan* 性善 "human nature is good." As was made clear, Mengzi did not mean by this that human beings are innately endowed with a complete and perfect moral sense, only that we are inclined toward goodness. As creatures, we have an affinity—a special innate *taste*—for morality.[2]

The next great figure in the Confucian tradition, Xunzi (310-219 B.C.E.), disagreed with Mengzi on this crucial issue of the character of human nature.[3] He advocated the alternative view that *xing'e* 性惡 "human nature is bad" and launched an overt attack on Mengzi's position. But we must explore the exact sense and implications of Xunzi's theory concerning the character of human nature, for these aspects of his thought have often been deeply misunderstood. This will prepare the way for a subsequent discussion of Xunzi's method of self cultivation.

The explicit debate between Xunzi and Mengzi marks the first documented, full-fledged disagreement within the emerging Confucian tradition. All vibrant traditions undergo this kind of internal debate as they struggle, in succeeding times and circumstances, to understand and apply the received teachings which they embrace. It seems fair to say that to participate in such a process of struggle and reinterpretation is a large part of what it means to be *in a tradition*.[4] In this regard, it is important to remember just how much Mengzi and Xunzi agreed about, for, at the end of the day, they were both Confucians. Indeed, in an important sense, their debate was about who really understood the tradition; though they disagreed about how to interpret Kongzi's teachings, they both looked to him as the source of and authority for their own views. They too turned to the past, just as Kongzi had before them and just as later Confucians would. But the difference is that both Mengzi and Xunzi and every Confucian who was to follow them explicitly claimed to be followers and defenders of Kongzi and his Way. This is why it makes sense to call them "Confucians."[5]

In terms of their ethical philosophies, Mengzi's and Xunzi's agreement went fairly deep; they do not seem to have disagreed much, if at all, about the character of moral action. That is to say, they did not, when faced with the same or similar situation, recommend different courses of action as right, as contemporary utilitarians and deontologists often do. Their views of the character of the sage, the fully cultivated person, seem to coincide in every important respect. Their disagreements concern the issues of what resources we possess when we begin the process of moral self cultivation and what the course of successful moral self cultivation is. In other words, they part company on the issues of the character of human nature and the process of moral education.[6]

In the course of Chinese history, Xunzi often has been criticized for what is considered to be his rather harsh view of human nature. This has led some traditional scholars to try to explain away his theory in one way or another. A prominent example of this phenomenon is Wang Xianqian (1842-1918), one of the foremost scholars and commentators on Xunzi. In the preface to his work  *Xunzi jijie* 荀子集解 "Collected Commentaries on the *Xunzi,*" Wang says,

> Formerly, during the Tang dynasty (618-907 C.E.), Han Yü regarded the *Xunzi* as a work with "many fine points and only a few blemishes." By the Song dynasty (960-1279 C.E.), those who attacked the text grew more numerous. If one were to infer the reason for this, it would be his teaching that human nature is bad. But I say that the notion that human nature is bad is not Xunzi's main point or fundamental idea. . . . I am saddened that Xunzi lived in an age of great chaos, when people were lost and confused, which moved him to come up with this theory.[7]

Here, Wang performs what we might call *psychological archeology* to uncover and explain the underlying motivation for Xunzi's theory. He claims that Xunzi was so distraught over the moral depravity of his age that he set forth this dour theory about human nature. However, Wang goes on to insist that, in some deep sense, this was not Xunzi's true view. He seems to say that this is how Xunzi *felt* about the people of his troubled age, but not how he *thought* about human nature *per se.*

More recent studies of Xunzi continue the attempt to "rehabilitate"

Xunzi's thought by explaining away his theory concerning human nature. This is done in at least two ways. First, there are those who argue that Xunzi's "pessimistic" theory complements Mengzi's more optimistic view of human nature.[8] They see Mengzi as cheerfully pointing out that our glass is half full (i.e., we are *partially good*), whereas Xunzi glumly focuses on the fact that our glass is half empty (i.e., we still are *half bad*). On such an interpretation, Mengzi offers an ideal toward which we are to strive, and is seen as encouraging us to develop the good already within us. Xunzi sets forth restrictions on our actions and warns us to curb our innate tendencies to err. A crucial feature of this position is the contention that the two views are *essentially* the same, differing only in what they emphasize.

Other scholars try to defuse the disagreement between Xunzi and Mengzi in another way, by claiming that they are talking at cross purposes. On this second view, Mengzi and Xunzi are simply using the word *xing* 性 "human nature" in different senses.[9] Mengzi uses the term to identify what is unique about human nature, as opposed to the nature of other creatures. This leads him to focus on the moral sense, argue that this describes our fundamental nature, and conclude that our nature is basically good. Xunzi, on the other hand, sees human nature in terms of its most basic and enduring features. This leads him to focus on our fundamental instincts, needs, and desires; argue that these constitute our fundamental nature; and conclude that our nature is basically bad.

These interpretations, like the earlier view of Wang Xianqian, seemed to be motivated largely by the desire to mend the rift in the Confucian family. They are based upon the important observation, noted above, that these two thinkers are, after all, Confucians, and must, therefore have much in common. But though this is true and an important point to keep in mind, these scholars have taken this idea too far. This leads them to claim that Mengzi and Xunzi have more in common than the evidence warrants. The unfortunate result is a misrepresentation of Xunzi's distinct and elegant position.[10]

Our understanding of Xunzi's theory of human nature has been obscured in other ways as well. For example, to some degree and in certain important respects, it was misunderstood and misrepresented by the justly famous sinologist, Homer H. Dubs.[11] However, Dubs's interpretation of Xunzi remains instructive, for seeing why it is wrong helps to bring important features of Xunzi's view into sharp relief and clear focus. Dubs claimed that Xunzi's position represents what I will refer to as an *Augustinian turn* in the Confucian tradition.[12] According to Dubs, Xunzi believed human nature was essentially *evil*. As a consequence, restraining the nature was Xunzi's first and highest priority. Moreover, Dubs correctly points out that Xunzi viewed Mengzi and his theory about the goodness of human nature as a dire threat to the Confucian Way; and so, Dubs contends, Xunzi devised the *xing'e* slogan (which Dubs understands as "human nature is evil") in order to counter the overly tender-hearted Mengzi.[13] Dubs sees this move by Xunzi as initiating an *authoritarian* theme in Chinese thought, a theme which he regards as the *de facto* dominant tendency in the Confucian tradition.

Despite the many merits of Dubs's analysis, the central claim of his interpretation is unfounded and misguiding. It is wholly unwarranted to ascribe to Xunzi, or any early Chinese thinker, the view that our nature, in whole or in part, is fundamentally and incorrigibly *evil*. There is nothing in Xunzi's thought that approaches the Augustinian notion of sin as an intentional rejection of God's will.[14] There is no hint in his writings that might lead one to think he believed we take a perverse *pleasure* in doing wrong.[15] This is an important point, for in order to have a position opposite to that of Mengzi in the way Dubs believes Xunzi's theory is, this is precisely what Xunzi would have to be saying.

These various interpretations miss the defining and most critical aspect of Xunzi's position; namely, that we begin life in a state of utter moral blindness. Morally, in our natural state, we are rudderless ships. According to Xunzi, we have no innate conception of what morality is; we would not recognize it even if we were to see it plainly before us. Prior to acquiring a proper education, moral categories simply are not part of our view of the world, any more than an appreciation of the notion of irony and the other beauties of literature is innately part of our nature. In the pre-social state of existence, we are led exclusively by our physical desires. In a world of limited goods, inhabited by creatures of more or less unlimited desires, it is inevitable that the result is destructive and alienating competition. This is what Xunzi means by his claim that human nature is bad.

In order to reform our bad nature, we must sign up for and successfully pursue a thorough, prolonged, and difficult course of learning. We must *re-form* our nature—as a warped board is re-formed by steam and pressure—so that it assumes a proper shape and can fit into the grand Confucian design.[16] This grand design is a plan for individuals, families, and society, that provides everyone with roles to fulfill, much as the score of a symphony describes for the members of an orchestra the different parts to play. The Confucian scheme was worked out over long periods of time by a series of gifted sages, through a process of trial and error. It alone provides the way to bring human needs and desires into a harmonious balance with Nature's capacity to produce goods.[17]

The learning that one must acquire consists of a thorough understanding of the various ritual practices and social obligations of Confucian society. Xunzi shared these with his rival Mengzi but viewed them very differently. Whereas Mengzi saw these practices and obligations as the refined manifestation of our nascent moral nature, Xunzi viewed them as wholly *artificial*, the accumulated wisdom of past sages. Xunzi employed a special term of art to capture this sense of the artificial nature of all society. The term is *wei* 偽 "deliberate action."[18]

One can see the difference between Mengzi's and Xunzi's views on human nature in the metaphors each thinker employs to convey his thought. Mengzi's moral sprouts and his repertoire of agricultural, *developmental* metaphors give way to a different set of images in Xunzi's *re-formation model*. At one point Xunzi says:

> Someone may ask: If human nature is bad, then where do rituals and social obligations come from? I would say, they all come from the *wei* "deliberate action" of the sages; essentially, they are not products of human nature. A potter molds clay and makes a vessel, but the vessel is the product of the deliberate action of the potter, not essentially a product of his nature. A carpenter carves a piece of wood and makes a utensil, but the utensil is the product of the deliberate action of the carpenter, not essentially a product of his nature. Sages gathered together their thoughts and ideas, experimented with various types of deliberate action and produced rituals and social obligations and set forth laws and regulations. Hence these are all products of the deliberate action of the sages, not essentially products of their nature.[19]

Xunzi sees morality itself as fundamentally artificial. Those who successfully pursue the course of study he recommends do not begin life with a moral sense which they go on to *develop*; they *acquire* a sensibility they never before had. It is true that all people possess the ability to acquire moral sensibility and also true that certain capacities that people possess at birth are more easily enlisted into the cause of morality and play a more critical role in keeping us on the moral path.[20] Nevertheless, until these innate abilities and capacities are given a proper and balanced shape, they tend to lead us into conflict rather than to morality. Even something as important in our ethical lives as our love for our children, if left undirected and unrefined, easily tends toward bad results. We need to pull hard against the promptings of our untutored nature in order to avoid vices such as nepotism and hold ourselves steady in order to move closer to what is right and proper .

According to Xunzi's view, those first embarking upon a study of the Way cannot really appreciate the moral dimensions of life. This is why they have great need not only for tradition but for teachers, who can guide them and help them to see and savor the many benefits available through the *Dao*.[21] Those who choose to study the Way are driven to it largely out of fear of the life they know and understand—the chaotic, dangerous, and profoundly unfulfilling life outside the Way.[22] Under the guidance of one who does understand, these students of the Way can come to appreciate more fully its simple and direct advantages. With further study, their understanding reaches the point where they begin to take profound satisfaction in virtue and ritual practice.

A comparison with the empiricist view of language acquisition may help to illustrate my understanding of Xunzi's view of how we come to have a moral sense of the world.[23] According to language empiricists, we begin life without language or any innate affinity to acquire natural languages. A person espousing this view of language acquisition might argue that when placed among competent language users, one acquires language purely as a tool in the service of one's basic needs and desires. But, as one is led to see and understand certain features about oneself and the world, instead of using language exclusively in an instrumental fashion—purely as a means to satisfy basic needs and desires—one may come to see it as intrinsically valuable, and as a new source of satisfaction. If our hypothetical language student has the necessary talent, training, energy, and luck, she may develop into a true poet—someone who regards the right kind of language as life itself. She would then achieve the literary equivalent of the Confucian sage; her love of and devotion to her art would mirror the sage's delight in and dedication to the Way.

An appreciation of literature—and this includes the wonder of it as a unique creation of human societies—is an *acquired taste*. Illiterate people simply (quite literally: *literally*) cannot understand these beauties; they see no meaning and find no satisfaction in the written word. This is why it is impossible to make a direct, compelling case to such individuals about the inherent value of such pursuits. One might appeal to the difficulty of getting around in society without knowing how to read. This is something such people know all too well. One could point out that literacy will increase their earning power—this is something everyone can understand. But one could not effectively appeal to the inherent value of literature. This is something one has to see from the inside of a life that includes such goods. On Xunzi's view, morality is like this, something the uninitiated can only understand in terms of its immediate usefulness in the quest to avoid harm and satisfy their basic desires; they have no innate *taste* for it, no *real* appreciation of it.

But, if people acquire enough knowledge about themselves and the world they inhabit, they will discover that there are new sources of profound satisfaction, beyond simply avoiding harm and fulfilling basic desires. There are things more valuable than life itself. The longer one studies, the more one understands, the deeper one's appreciation of the

Way will be. The culmination of this process is a fundamental change in one's evaluative scheme. It is not that one no longer recognizes the good of avoiding harm or that one no longer takes satisfaction in fulfilling basic desires, but one sees these through a more powerful lens that reveals their true proportion in a larger picture of the good life. In the initial stages of self cultivation, knowledge of the Way will enable one to override one's errant desires. As one's understanding deepens and, with sustained and concerted practice, one shapes oneself to the moral way, one discovers new, richer, and more powerful sources of satisfaction within a newly unfolding form of life. At this point, the initial tension between what one desires and what is right weakens; one finds additional motivation to do what is right and one comes to see how many of one's basic desires not only can be satisfied but enhanced in a well-lived life.[24] If one succeeds in becoming a sage, one will no longer need to struggle against recalcitrant desires, for one's desires will be in complete accord with what is right.

As one reads the *Xunzi*, one is struck by the low opinion he has of human beings in their pre-social state.[25] But this only serves to increase his reverence for their achievements. When human beings get things right, things are *really* right. He expresses nothing less than a religious reverence for culture, which for him has as its core the Confucian rites. At one point he says,

> Through the rites Heaven and earth join in harmony,  the sun and the moon shine, the four seasons proceed in order, the stars and constellations march, the rivers flow, and all things flourish; people's likes and dislikes are regulated and their joys and hates made appropriate. Those below are obedient, those above are enlightened; all things move through their various changes but do not become disordered; only those who turn their backs upon the rites will be destroyed. Are the rites not wonderful indeed! [26]

Xunzi believed, and here he seems to be largely correct, that most of the valuable things we experience or know of are things that we have *acquired* through the good fortune of living in the right kinds of societies, and that we are largely unaware of the debt we owe to those whose fruits we now enjoy. He saw Mengzi's claim that we all possess an innate moral sense as a Promethean arrogance, a delusion that would have disastrous results. Such a view would lead people to ignore the wisdom of the sages and their hard-wrought insights and follow the false and fickle light of an imaginary moral sense.[27] Mengzi's theory of human nature would lead people to believe that they knew more than they could possibly know, relying only upon their innate intuitions.

Although Xunzi has a rather dim view of our nature, he is tremendously optimistic and has great confidence in our ability to transform that nature.[28] He shares this profound optimism with Mengzi; both believed in the fundamental perfectibility of human beings.[29] However, their views on the nature of the process leading to this state differ considerably. Mengzi's view of moral self cultivation describes the process as a natural flowering or *development* of inherent tendencies. Xunzi sees it as the difficult and demanding task of acquiring a second nature. For Xunzi, successful self cultivation requires protracted and concerted effort, for the task is to constrain and *re-form* a recalcitrant and unruly nature.[30]

Again, the differences between Mengzi and Xunzi are clearly visible in the images they each invoke. Gone is Mengzi's patient farmer, the devoted cultivator, and in her place is an artisan, working in a difficult medium. Xunzi says:

> A piece of wood as straight as a plumb line may [with soaking and shaping] be bent into a circle as true as any drawn with a compass, and once the wood has dried it will not straighten out again. The process of bending has made it that way. Thus, if [crooked] wood is placed against a straightening board, it can be made straight; if metal is put to the grindstone, it can be sharpened; and if the gentleman studies widely and each day examines himself, his wisdom will become clear and his conduct without fault.[31]

This passage might remind one of Kant's remark: *Aus so krummem Holze, als woraus der Mensch gemacht ist, kann nichts ganz Gerades gezimmert werden.* "One cannot hope to make anything perfectly straight out of such crooked timber as man is made."[32] But, as noted above, while Xunzi shares this rather dim view of our *nature,* he is much more optimistic about the possibility of working this raw material into something that is without flaw. Xunzi assures us that with enough work of the right sort, we can straighten the crooked timber of humanity in a way that will ensure that it will remain straight. He expresses this idea by way of a different metaphor—borrowed from the *Odes*—saying that we can transform our rough and unformed nature into a precious and unblemished gem.[33] Another important difference from Kant is that Xunzi looked to the tried and true methods of past sages—social practices and obligations that had evolved over the course of human history—instead of pure reason as his standard and guide.

Xunzi thought one could transform one's nature and achieve a state in which one would no longer be in tension with one's "lower self." Once one had "bent" one's nature into the proper form, it retained this shape without further struggle. But this did not come without great effort. As noted earlier, it required, above all else, profound perseverance and singleness of purpose. As Xunzi says:

Those who miss one shot in a hundred cannot be called really good archers. Those who set out on a thousand-mile journey and break down half a pace from the destination cannot be called really good carriage drivers. Those who do not comprehend moral relationships and categories and who do not make themselves one with benevolence and righteousness cannot be called really good scholars. Learning basically means to achieve this oneness.[34]

The process Xunzi describes does not have at its core an innate moral sense that, by its natural delight in morality and revulsion to what is bad, provides us with a weak yet persistent moral guide. The course of moral self cultivation is not a process of *developing* innate "moral sprouts." According to Xunzi, we cannot steer by our own internal light, for this light is not yet lit. The illumination of morality is something we must *acquire*; it is something handed down from the sages. As a consequence and in contrast to what Mengzi taught, reflecting upon one's intuitions is not a prominent element of Xunzi's program of moral education. He provides very different counsel. We are to keep ourselves focused on the task of learning. Referring to the notions of *si* "reflection" and *xue* "learning," which serve as a central theme of this study, Xunzi tells us:

I once spent a whole day in *si* "reflection," but I found it of less value than a moment of *xue* "learning." I once tried standing on tiptoe and gazing into the distance, but I found I could see much farther by climbing to a high place.[35]

Xunzi's high place was the edifice of culture which, as human beings, is our unique and precious inheritance. His advice was to climb to this high place by following the steep and rugged path of learning. He believed it was a long and arduous climb, but he also believed it afforded a vast and incomparable view.

# Notes

1. In this context, I mean by "moral luck" whether or not one happens to be born in an age when the Way is flourishing, in a state that propagates it and, in a family that nurtures and cultivates one's moral inclinations. These are monumentally important factors that for most people will decide the course of their moral lives but which seem wholly a matter of good or bad fortune. The analysis of moral luck in the west tends to be focused more on individual actions and their consequences. For example, see Thomas Nagel, "Moral Luck" in *Mortal Questions* reprint (London: Cambridge University Press, 1982), Martha C. Nussbaum, *The Fragility of Goodness* (London: Cambridge

University Press, 1986) and Bernard Williams, "Moral Luck" in *Moral Luck* (London: Cambridge University Press, 1986).

2. Mengzi himself likens the cultivated moral sense to the palate of a connoisseur of fine food or music in 6A7. Cf. 6A10.

3. The dates for Xunzi's life are from John Knoblock, "The Chronology of Xunzi's Works," *Early China*, 8 (1982-1983): 29-52. Professor Knoblock has also produced a complete translation and study of the text. See his *Xunzi: A Translation and Study of the Complete Works* (Stanford, CA: Stanford University Press (vol. 1, 1988; vol. 2, 1990; vol. 3, 1994). For a general study of Xunzi's thought, see Paul R. Goldin, *Rituals of the Way: The Philosophy of Xunzi* (Chicago: Open Court, 1999).

4. For an enlightening discussion of the internal struggles traditions undergo, which uses the contemporary west as an example, see Alasdair MacIntyre, *After Virtue* (Notre Dame, IN: University of Notre Dame Press, 1984). In his later work, MacIntyre goes on to explore how different traditions, which define competing forms of rationality, can still interact and challenge one another. See his *Whose Justice? Which Rationality?* (Notre Dame, IN: University of Notre Dame Press, 1984) and *Three Rival Versions of Moral Enquiry: Encyclopedia, Genealogy and Tradition* (Notre Dame, IN: University of Notre Dame Press, 1990). One of the most revealing accounts of how traditions inform human lives with persisting value is Edward Shils, *Tradition* (Chicago: University of Chicago Press, 1981). T. C. Kline has done an impressive job applying the insights of Shils and others to the specific case of Xunzi. See his "Moral Agency and Motivation in the *Xunzi*" in Kline and Ivanhoe, *Virtue, Nature, and Moral Agency in the Xunzi*.

5. Some members of the tradition might be seen as presenting challenges to this generalization. For example, Wang Yangming, whose views we examine below, insisted that he had greater trust in his own moral mind than the words of Kongzi. But even Wang expressed his allegiance to Kongzi's Way and like other Confucians referred to him as *the* sage and teacher.

6. This is an important point and not only for understanding the differences between Mengzi and Xunzi. Several contemporary accounts of the nature of virtue suffer because they do not clearly distinguish the abilities and dispositions of highly cultivated individuals from those who are, to varying degrees, undeveloped. This leads some philosophers to talk about abilities like moral sensitivity and discernment as if they were innate faculties rather than largely acquired dispositions. While Mengzi and Xunzi disagree about how much is acquired, neither of them makes the mistake of seeing moral sensitivity or discrimination as fully formed, innate faculties. However, as we shall see, later Confucians, for example Wang Yangming, do make this kind of claim. John McDowell offers a good example of a contemporary philosopher who makes this type of mistake (in the course of many fascinating observations). He repeatedly deploys a set of ocular metaphors to describe moral perception and these obscure rather than make clear important issues

about human nature and the course of moral development. See his, "Values and Secondary Qualities," in Geoffrey Sayre-McCord, ed., *Essays on Moral Realism* (Ithaca, NY: Cornell University Press, 1988): 166-80, and "Are Moral Requirements Hypothetical Imperatives?" *Proceedings of the Aristotelian Society, Supplementary Volume 52* (1978): 13-29.

7. Wang Xianqian 王先謙, *Xunzi jijie* 荀子集解 (Changsha, 1891). Wang's reference is to Han Yü's 韓愈 (768-824 C.E.) work *Du Xun* 讀荀 "Reading the *Xunzi*." See *Han Changli quanji* 韓昌黎全集 11:15a-b (*SBBY*).

8. The clearest proponent of this view is Antonio S. Cua. See his *Ethical Argumentation: A Study in Hsün Tzu's Moral Epistemology* (Honolulu: University of Hawaii Press, 1985): 15 and *passim*. I have benefitted from the unpublished work of Derek Fung Ling on this aspect of Xunzi's ethical thought.

9. For example, see D. C. Lau, "Theories of Human Nature in Mengzi and Xunzi" in Kline and Ivanhoe, *Virtue, Nature, and Moral Agency in the Xunzi*.

10. The assumption which leads all of these later scholars astray is that belonging to a tradition is a matter of sharing certain core doctrines. Rather, belonging to a tradition is a matter of sharing a canon and being part of an ongoing, developing dialogue. Cf. MacIntyre on this issue. (I owe this observation to Bryan W. Van Norden.)

11. Homer H. Dubs, "Mencius and Sun-dz on Human Nature" *Philosophy East and West* 6 (1965): 213-22.

12. Dubs himself likens Xunzi's position to that of Augustine. See "Mencius and Sun-dz," p. 216.

13. This aspect of Dubs' view is well justified. Xunzi wrote an entire essay dedicated to refuting Mengzi's view of human nature, raising a number of arguments against its plausibility and pointing out the dire consequences such a theory could precipitate. Moreover, Xunzi's theory that human nature is bad can be seen as a background assumption supporting many other claims he makes throughout his writings. For a translation of Xunzi's "Human Nature Is Bad" chapter, see Burton Watson, tr., *Hsün Tzu: Basic Writings* (New York: Columbia University Press, 1963): 157-71.

14. As Joel Kupperman astutely points out, Augustinian-style views presuppose a *knowledge* of the good that Xunzi's view explicitly rejects. See his "Xunzi: Morality as Psychological Constraint" in Kline and Ivanhoe, *Virtue, Nature, and Moral Agency in the Xunzi*.

15. Compare this with Augustine's description of stealing pears with his friends, ". . . (we) carried away great loads, not to eat ourselves, but to fling to the very swine, having only eaten some of them; and to do this pleased us all the more because it was not permitted . . . I should be gratuitously wanton, having no inducement to evil but the evil itself. It was

foul and I loved it. I loved to perish. I loved my own error—not that for which I erred, but the error itself. Base soul, falling from Thy firmament to utter destruction—not seeking aught through the shame but the shame itself!" *The Confessions* in *Basic Writings of Saint Augustine*, Whitney J. Oates, tr. (New York: Random House, 1948): 24.

16. My use of the term *re-formation* is intended to distinguish Xunzi's type of moral education from Mengzi's developmental model. Jonathan W. Schofer was the first to articulate this difference. He explores this aspect of Xunzi's thought, as well as others, in his lucid and insightful article, "Virtues in Xunzi's Thought" in Kline and Ivanhoe, *Virtue, Nature, and Moral Agency in the Xunzi*.

17. I describe this feature of Xunzi's philosophy in "A Happy Symmetry: Xunzi's Ethical Thought," *Journal of the American Academy of Religion* 59.2 (Summer, 1991): 309-22. For an incisive study of Xunzi's social and political views, see Henry Rosemont, Jr., "State and Society in the *Xunzi*: A Philosophical Commentary" in Kline and Ivanhoe, *Virtue, Nature, and Moral Agency in the Xunzi*.

18. It is not clear whether Xunzi actually devised a new character for this notion, i.e., adding the "human" radical to the character meaning "to do," or whether this graphic distinction was the work of later scholars. But Xunzi surely used the word in precise and novel ways. In the "Rectifying Names" chapter he provides two related yet distinct senses of the term *wei*: (1) individual intentional actions and (2) dispositions or critical habits developed through repeated intentional actions. In modern Chinese, the word *wei* retains the sense of "artificial." In modern usage, it also has the connotation of something that is "false," a sense not present in Xunzi's original use of the term.

19. Adapted from Watson, *Hsün Tzu: Basic Writings*, p. 160.

20. David Wong was the first to make this aspect of Xunzi's philosophy fully explicit. See his "Xunzi on Moral Motivation" in Kline and Ivanhoe, *Virtue, Nature, and Moral Agency in the Xunzi*. T. C. Kline provides the clearest account of such innate tendencies and describes them as parts of our nature that through practice of the Way can be "conscripted" into the cause of morality. See his "Moral Agency and Motivation in the *Xunzi*."

21. By comparison, the role and importance of tradition and teachers are not prominent themes in the writings of Mengzi.

22. Of course there are certain straightforward goods associated with a life according to the Way. Under normal circumstances the moral person enjoys a broad range of material, social, and psychological goods. Many of these can be understood by the uninitiated as well and provide some motivation to undertake a study of the Way. But Xunzi tends to focus on the order, security, and safety afforded by the Way and oppose this to the chaotic, precarious, and perilous life outside the Way. Perhaps this is because he felt that if someone was motivated exclusively or even primarily by more mundane

concerns, they would not be able to withstand the demands and sacrifices necessary to master the Way.

23. Much of my discussion of the difference between language empiricists and language innatists is based upon the analysis to be found in Ian Hacking, *Why Does Language Matter to Philosophy?* reprint (London: Cambridge University Press, 1990): 57-69.

24. For example, one can satisfy one's basic desire for sex in a richer and more meaningful way through a sustained and mutually respectful relationship than through wanton promiscuity. One can satisfy a desire for adventure and danger in more complex and fulfilling ways by serving in some socially worthy cause that involves chance and risk.

25. The opening of the "Discussion of Rites" chapter presents a picture of the pre-social state that is worthy of Hobbes's well-turned phrase: "solitary, poor, nasty, brutish and short."

26. Watson, *Hsün Tzu: Basic Writings*, p. 94.

27. Xunzi states this explicitly in the "Human Nature Is Bad" chapter. See Watson, *Hsün Tzu: Basic Writings*, pp. 162-3.

28. Whereas Hobbes assumes that people have the capacity to devise and enter into contracts, Xunzi argues that we can escape the state of nature because we have a capacity for self-transformation. Such a capacity rests upon the human ability to make distinctions and evaluate among them (for example, see the chapter "Against Physiognomy") and to organize themselves in different ways (for example, see the chapter "The Regulations of a King").

29. This is one important way in which they differ from many western thinkers. In particular, it distinguishes Xunzi from thinkers like Hobbes or Freud, with whom he shares certain similarities. Since Xunzi believes that one can *transform* oneself in fundamental ways, he can avoid certain classic difficulties encountered by thinkers like Hobbes, who offer contractarian ethical philosophies. Since the process of self cultivation transforms the self and changes the calculus by which one decides what one is to do, Xunzi avoids the set of problems associated with "prisoner's dilemma" situations.

30. Thus for Xunzi, the most important virtues a beginning student can have are singleness of purpose and tenacity. This is a consistent theme of Xunzi's and is prominent in the opening chapter of the text, "Encouraging Learning." Elsewhere, I have argued that in this respect Xunzi is much closer to Kongzi than is Mengzi. See my "Thinking and Learning In Early Confucianism." Also, see Schofer's article (cited above in note 16) for an incisive discussion of the nature of virtue in Xunzi's thought and this issue in particular.

31. Adapted from Watson, *Hsün Tzu: Basic Writings*, p. 15.

32. Immanuel Kant, "Idee zu einer allgemeinen Geschichte in weltbürgerlicher Absicht" (1784). For a complete translation of this essay,

see Patrick Gardiner, ed., *Theories of History* (Glencoe, IL: The Free Press, 1959): 22-34.

33. In chapter 27, Xunzi follows Kongzi by employing a quote from the *Odes* to make an analogy between self cultivation and the art of lapidary. He says, "Human beings are to the study of culture as jade is to cutting and polishing. And so the *Odes* says, 'Like cutting, like filing, like grinding, like polishing.'" See *Analects* 1.15 for the same idea. Cf. pp. 3-4.

34. Adapted from Watson, *Hsün Tzu: Basic Writings*, p. 22.

35. Adapted from Watson, *Hsün Tzu: Basic Writings*, p. 16. In this passage, Xunzi paraphrases Kongzi. For the similar passage in the *Analects,* see 15.31. Compare Xunzi's view with that of Kongzi, as described in chapter 1, pages 2-3. I discuss this issue in considerable detail and in relation to Mengzi's thought in "Thinking and Learning in Early Confucianism."

朱熹

# 4. Zhu Xi

Zhu Xi (1130-1200 C.E.) is without doubt the most influential Chinese thinker since the classical age, and understanding his thought is essential for anyone who seeks to understand subsequent Chinese history.[1] One could offer a number of explanations for why Zhu had such a profound, pervasive, and persistent effect on later Chinese thought, but among the most important reasons of all are his sheer brilliance and remarkable industry.[2] A combination of genius and diligence enabled him to bring together the various strands of texts, practices, and ideas that had accumulated around the Confucian tradition and weave them into a powerful and coherent system of thought.[3] He stands as one of the greatest synthesizers in world history.

Several scholars[4] have likened Zhu Xi to Aquinas, and in certain respects such a comparison is neither unwarranted nor unrevealing. As an interpreter of an earlier master, Mengzi, Zhu does resemble Aquinas's relationship to Aristotle. But, in other respects, such a comparison is inappropriate and can be misleading. For example, Zhu Xi fully identified with Mengzi, philosophically, personally, and spiritually, in a way Aquinas did not and could not identify with the pagan, Aristotle. Zhu Xi saw himself as *replaying* the role of his fellow Confucian Mengzi in his own time, fighting against Daoism and Buddhism, and keeping the Jin "barbarians" at bay, just as Mengzi had fought Yang and Mo and kept the "barbarians" of his own time from overrunning China.[5] In these and other regards, the comparison with Aquinas breaks down.

But though Zhu Xi saw himself as fighting off the twin banes of Daoism and Buddhism, his thought was deeply influenced by these two traditions, often in ways of which he was unaware. Both in what he inherited from earlier Neo-Confucian thinkers and in his own philosophizing, Zhu employed a set of concepts and a way of thinking that finds few if any parallels in the thought of early Confucians such as Mengzi. The origin of these new concepts and ways of thinking can be traced to the accumulated influence of Daoism and Buddhism; the terms of art and philosophical styles of these grand traditions came to dominate the Chinese intellectual scene in the period between the first and eighth centuries. In turn, these traditions and the ways of thinking associated with them were transformed as they were synthesized by Chinese intellectuals. Zhu Xi saw the world, himself, and his tradition in these new, hybrid terms and categories.

Zhu Xi developed and made clear the views of earlier Neo-Confucian thinkers, notably Cheng Yi (1033-1107 C.E.),[6] in ways that helped to reestablish the preeminence of the Confucian tradition. In particular, Zhu's new views on human nature and the mind enabled him to provide

43

a "solution" to what was a perennial Confucian problem: reconciling the claim that human nature is good with the all-too-evident bad behavior of large numbers of people. But with the rise of a new and radical conception of what it meant for human nature to be "good," this perennial problem became increasingly pronounced and pressing in the Song dynasty. In order to appreciate this and other aspects of Zhu Xi's thought and the views of the later Confucian philosophers we will examine, it is necessary to have some grasp of the complex set of metaphysical ideas and theories that came to dominate Chinese philosophical thought of this period. The presentation here is compact and selective; we will focus only on those facets of this broad and complicated interaction that bear directly on our guiding concern: moral self cultivation. In particular, we will explore some of the ways in which Neo-Confucian views of human nature and the mind were influenced by Daoist and Buddhist ideas, and how Zhu Xi incorporated such ideas into his own philosophical system.[7]

Early Buddhists[8] believed that all suffering (and every other imperfect aspect of the world), arises ultimately as a result of mistaken views about the self and the nature of reality. Specifically, early Buddhists claim that most people fail to realize that the self and the things in the world are fundamentally "empty"; i.e., they do not exist independently and they do not endure. The belief in an independent and enduring self or soul is particularly problematic, for it generates desires that, given the nature of things, are impossible to satisfy. Simply put, we believe that we and the things we desire endure, but in fact we and all things are in a constant state of coming into and passing out of being. Nothing lasts. But, because of our belief in an independent and enduring self, we crave such continuity. And so, these false views about the self and reality inevitably result in incessant and unending dissatisfaction and deepening and more damaging ignorance.

The way out of this sad state is to develop right views about the self and the world, to see the true nature of reality. One with right views realizes that the desires that had tormented her ultimately are *unreal* (i.e., "empty"), they don't correspond to anything out there in the world, and that she too is unreal, only a temporary phenomenon, the result of the accumulated effects of past causes and conditions. Such a realization has the power to relieve the incessant feeling of dissatisfaction that is thought inevitably to haunt those who cling to the delusion of an independent and enduring self.

Through its interaction with indigenous Chinese thought, particularly Daoism, Buddhism underwent considerable changes.[9] One such change bears directly on our present concern. The early Buddhist notion that all the imperfect aspects of reality are ultimately unreal became transformed into the idea that our less savory aspects are not *really* part of our nature. In other words, certain of our desires—those that lead to strife and dissatisfaction—are thought to be not *unreal* but *unnatural*.

As a consequence of this shift in view, Chinese thinkers gradually modified the Buddhist understanding of emptiness and in a sense filled it in with a more robust picture. The things of the world, and of course this included the self, were still fundamentally empty of independent and enduring being, but this now was seen as a consequence of their sharing a common, fundamental nature: a lively, caring, transpersonal Buddha-nature. Ignorance of the true nature of the self was still the cause of all suffering, but now ignorance was conceived of as the failure to realize that Buddha-nature is our true nature.[10]

The Buddhist project, particularly in the Chan school (more commonly known in the west by its Japanese name, Zen), became the discovery and release of one's inherent Buddha-nature. This was accomplished by paring away the selfish desires and false views that obscure this lively, innate, and perfect nature. In the language of texts like the *Platform Sutra*, one needs to clean one's spiritual mirror.[11] One does this by realizing that the "dust" obscuring one's mirror—and the mirror itself—are nothing more than self-generated, self-imposed, and self-sustained delusions. These obscurations are empty or unreal, in the sense that they are not *natural*.[12] Such deformations and delusions would simply disappear if only we could fully engage and bring into spontaneous play our true and fundamental nature.

However, though they themselves are ultimately unreal, these delusions have very severe consequences. For just as the illusion of a motion picture can cause one to feel very real fear, anger, or sorrow, these false views about the self and the world cause deluded individuals to hate and fear, lust and grieve. And since the objects of these emotional disturbances are not real, such people have no hope of finding satisfaction regarding them. The only way to escape from this most unsatisfactory state is to realize the true nature of the self and the world. We must realize that in our natural or original state, the self is fundamentally connected to every aspect of reality, we are all aspects of the universal Buddha-nature. This realization has the power to relieve our former distress and anxiety, since we are no longer alienated from and opposed to a world of "others" and "objects." Such an understanding gives rise to a feeling of profound peace and universal compassion toward all sentient beings.

The image of the mind as a mirror, or alternatively, as the calm surface of a body of water which reflects all things perfectly, is not original to Buddhism, it comes from the *Zhuangzi*.[13] When Zhuangzi says that the sage "uses his mind like a mirror"[14] he means that the sage reacts to the world in perfect harmony with the way it is by allowing his innate nature to spontaneously and pre-reflectively manifest itself. This view of human nature deeply influenced the notion of Buddha-nature which developed among Chinese Buddhists and this, in turn, had a profound influence on Neo-Confucian conceptions of human nature. In particular, all three traditions tended to see human nature as having two fundamental aspects: a pure, original mode and an adulterated, instantiated mode. Neo-Confucians began to talk about an "original nature" and a "material nature." The former is perfect and complete, the latter flawed and in need of refinement.

Under the influence of these new, hybrid notions, Mengzi's claim about the original goodness of human nature came to be understood as referring to the original, perfect, and pure state of human nature—not to certain of its nascent tendencies. In his profoundly influential commentary on the *Mengzi*, Zhu Xi interpreted Mengzi's term *duan* 端 "sprout [of goodness]" as *xu* 緒 a "clue" or "indication" of what the underlying nature was *really* like.[15] He came to see self cultivation not as the *development* of incipient tendencies but as the *recovery* or release of this "original nature" by refining one's imperfect and obscuring "material nature."

In order to fill out Zhu Xi's *recovery model* of moral self cultivation, we need to describe two additional central terms of art and see how he used these to explain his theory of human nature and the mind. The first term, *li* 理 "pattern" or "principle," in early Daoist thought, meant the underlying patterns and processes that run throughout the world. Different things contribute to these patterns and processes and possess their own individual structures, which are parts of this larger, grand scheme. Under the influence of Buddhist philosophy, this notion of *li* changed dramatically. Most importantly, the underlying structure of the universe came to be seen as *completely present* in every mote of dust.[16] Each aspect of reality was thought to reflect all the other aspects, and so all the world was present in each and every particle of it.[17] However, for reasons that will be explained below, Neo-Confucians believed that a given thing only manifests certain particular *li* and this is what makes the thing the kind of thing it is.

For Neo-Confucian thinkers, *li* is both descriptive and normative; when things follow *li* they are as they ought to be, i.e., they are *natural*. When things do not follow *li* they are "deviant" or "perverse." *Li* is present in and provides the proper standard for all things, plant or animal, living or inert. Consider the following question and Zhu Xi's response:

[Question] "*Li* 'principle' is what is received from Heaven by both human beings and other creatures. Do things without feelings also possess principle?"

[Answer] "Of course they have principle. For example, a ship can go on water while a cart can go only on land."[18]

*Li* gives form and meaning to all things but is itself without perceptible form or meaning. In order to possess either, it must be embedded in *qi* 氣 "energy" or "lively matter."[19] *Qi* is that of which the world is made. It is not inert matter, and it comes in various grades of impurity. The purer, more "limpid" *qi* tends to rise, is warm and active. Impure, "murky" *qi* tends to sink, and is cool and lethargic. The *qi* of different things, to varying degrees, obscures the *li* within them and only allows some of it to shine through. So while all things equally possess all the *li*, their different endowments of *qi* make them different, since each thing only manifests certain of the *li*. Moreover, given that *qi* exists in different grades of purity and is constantly churning around, when people are generated out of *qi*, their endowments naturally differ in purity. One's individual endowment is referred to as one's *cai* 才 "capacity" or "talent," and this determines, at least to begin with, how aware one is of the various principles in the world. Those with a better endowment of *qi* are naturally "clearer" about how things are. The purer one's *qi*, the more *li* shines forth and the more one understands.

[Someone asked] "Human beings and other creatures all receive the *li* of Heaven and earth to serve as their nature and the *qi* of Heaven and earth to serve as their physical shape. The reason people have different characters is because [their *qi*] has different degrees of turbidity or purity. [But] in the case of other creatures, I do not know whether the difference is due to their endowment of *li* being incomplete or whether it is the result of obscurity and obstruction of their endowment of *qi*."

[Zhu Xi replied] "Their limited capabilities are all due to the *qi* which they receive. For example, take dogs or horses. Their physical constitution being what it is, they are only capable of certain activities."[20]

Since each thing possesses all the *li*, in theory at least, each and every thing is innately endowed with perfect knowledge. But human beings are unique among things in that we alone have the ability to realize this knowledge completely by refining our *qi* to a highly tenuous state which allows all the *li* to shine forth. Most important, this allows us to realize complete and perfect knowledge of moral "patterns" or "principles." This endowment, something like a complete set of innate ideas,[21] is our basic *xing* 性 "nature." But, as I mentioned earlier, Neo-Confucians introduced a novel twist by positing a distinction between our *benxing* 本性 "original nature," which is *li* in itself, and our our *qizhi zhi xing* 氣質之 性 "material nature," which is *li* embedded in *qi*. Zhu Xi often does not explicitly distinguish when he is talking about our "original" as opposed to our "material" nature, but what he means is almost always clear from context. In the following passage, he is very specific and presents an excellent summation of the ideas I have been discussing.

> [Someone asked] "Since material nature differs in its degree of impurity, [is it not the case that] there are partial and complete endowments of Heavenly nature?"
> [Zhu Xi replied] "It is not the case that there are partial and complete [endowments of Heavenly nature]. It is like the light of the sun or the moon. If one is on open ground then one sees all of the light, but if one is inside a thatched hut, then some of the light is blocked and obscured, some is seen while some is not. The impurity results from an impurity of the *qi*, so naturally there is obstruction, as if one were inside a thatched hut. But in the case of human beings, it is possible to penetrate the blockage and obstruction. As for animals, they too have this same nature, but it is restricted by their physical constitutions which produce blockage and obstruction that is so severe, it cannot be penetrated. As for the benevolence manifested by tigers and wolves,[22] the sacrifices performed by jackals and otters and the proper social norms followed by bees and ants, these are the few places where they are able to penetrate their innate blockage and obstruction, like a thin shaft of light shining through a crack. As for apes, since their physical form is similar to human beings, they are the most intelligent of animals, only lacking the ability to speak."[23]

Corresponding to the two aspects or modes of "original" and "material" nature, Zhu Xi describes two aspects or modes of mind, *daoxin* 道心 "the mind of the Way" and *renxin* 人心 "the human mind."[24] As we cultivate ourselves, we move from the latter mode to the former; we clarify the *qi* in which the mind is embedded until the principles therein shine forth, suspended and unobstructed in the most rarefied of *qi*. Other creatures have lesser levels of awareness of *li* as a direct result of their "denser" endowments of *qi* which, unfortunately, they cannot refine. This spectrum of awareness passes down through plants to inanimate objects whose *qi* is so dense that they lack any degree of consciousness at all. Human beings, as noted earlier, are uniquely able to refine their *qi* and move from relative ignorance to a complete and comprehensive knowledge of the world. But this knowledge is something they already have within them; the process of refining one's *qi* allows one to recover this inherent knowledge.[25]

Zhu Xi's *recovery model* of self cultivation can be viewed as having two primary aspects and a mediating state which unites them. The first aspect consists of *cunxin* 存心 "preserving the mind" by *zun dexing* 尊德 性 "honoring the virtuous nature."[26] The practice of *jingzuo* 靜坐 "quiet sitting" was the primary method for carrying out this half of the task.[27] The goal was to gather together and calm one's mind, and thereby protect it from the obscuring effects of agitated emotions and desires.[28] In a calm state of mind, one's *qi* tended to settle and the principles of the mind were more easily brought into awareness and manifested. But, as important as this practice was, it alone would not advance one's grasp of principle, and quiet sitting could become a liability to moral progress if one allowed it to become an end unto itself. In order to supplement this practice and guard against the slide into quietism, Zhu Xi advocated a second component, *dao wenxue* 道問學 "pursuing inquiry and study." This half of the task consisted primarily of a practice called *gewu* 格物 "investigating things," which meant studying, on the one hand, the classical texts of Confucianism and, on the other, the various events and phenomena one encounters in the course of daily life—all with the aim of grasping the ruling *li* behind these objects of investigation.[29]

Uniting both these halves of the task of self cultivation was the attitude of *jing* 敬 "reverential attention."[30] This state of mind was to be maintained throughout self cultivation, whether engaged in the task of "preserving the mind" or "pursuing inquiry and study." It is difficult to say exactly what this state of mind is like, but perhaps it is best to think of reverential attention as an attitude of calm perseverance, seriousness, and reflection in the midst of the ongoing activity of self cultivation.

One of the great strengths of Zhu Xi's method of self cultivation is that it provided students of the Way with a definite procedure and clear criteria for study. The very idea that one must engage in self cultivation implies the need for some standard, other than one's own spontaneous intuitions. But to what standard does one appeal and how is one to approach this task? Earlier Confucians faced a similar problem, though with much different metaphysical and epistemological assumptions. As we have seen, they appealed to the traditional rites as well as to a set of classical texts.[31] And yet, even among these early Confucians, there was a heated debate, most notably represented by the disagreement between Mengzi and Xunzi, concerning how much of moral self cultivation involved *intuiting* knowledge through a process of thinking or reflecting, as opposed to *acquiring* it through a course of learning. As will become clear, the disagreement between Zhu Xi and Wang Yangming, the next thinker we will discuss, can be seen as a retelling of this debate in the very different philosophical language of Neo-Confucianism.

Zhu Xi relied heavily on his interpretation of the texts of Neo-Confucianism to provide clear criteria to students of the Way, and he arranged these texts into a systematic course of study, thus providing them with a definite program of learning. One was first to study the *Four Books:* the *Daxue, Zhongyong, Mengzi,* and *Analects.*[32] Next, one was to study the original *Five Classics:* the *History, Rites, Odes, Spring and Autumn Annals,* and *Changes.* Only the first and third of these were among the texts of our earlier Confucian thinkers, though Xunzi may also have used some version of the second. The third stage of study consisted of a careful reading of the official dynastic histories, which of course did not exist prior to the Han dynasty and hence were unknown to Kongzi, Mengzi, and Xunzi. The three stages of Zhu Xi's curriculum were thought to represent specific aspects of his program of learning: first, *theory;* next, *paradigmatic cases;* and finally, more general and extensive *applications.* Within each of these stages were subdivisions. For example, of the *Four Books,* one was to begin with the *Daxue.* Quoting Cheng Yi, Zhu Xi's introductory remarks on the *Daxue* begin:

> The *Daxue* is a surviving work of the Confucian school and is the gate through which the beginning student enters into virtue. It is only due to the preservation of this work that the order in which the ancients pursued their learning may be seen at this time.[33]

The *Daxue* was an obscure chapter from a larger work called the *Liji* "Rites" until it was elevated to canonical status during the Song dynasty.[34] In this process, the original text was altered significantly, first by Cheng Yi and then again by Zhu Xi. These changes included adding material to the original text, but perhaps the most important change concerned the reordering of part of the text. Zhu propagated a version that put *gewu* "the investigation of things" before *chengyi* 誠意 "making one's thoughts sincere." This was one of the central issues of contention between Zhu Xi's school and what was to become the Lu-Wang School.[35] Essentially, the ordering Zhu follows suggests that one must first acquire an understanding of *li,* through the process of *gewu* "the investigation of things," and then through *jing* "reverential attention" to these principles, one comes to *chengyi* "make one's thoughts sincere," i.e., embody the *li* in every thought, feeling, and action. A more charitable reading would insist that, for Zhu Xi, the process of making one's thoughts sincere occurs *as* one investigates things *with* an attitude of reverential attention.

By anchoring his learning in the mastery of a corpus of texts, Zhu Xi sought to avoid an overreliance upon individual intuition, which he perceived as posing the danger of drifting into radical subjectivism. This was his central criticism of Lu Xiangshan's approach. Zhu sought to set up a standard which could be used to judge between competing claims regarding the true course of the *Dao*, and then determine which claims were correct. It might seem that what he recommends simply pushes the criterion up one level, for people can always discover that they disagree over what the texts mean. Zhu Xi was aware of this, and had several responses. First, his program of learning required one to apply one's interpretation of the classics to the actual affairs of life. He believed that this requirement would winnow out erroneous interpretations, for those that accorded with the *Dao* would work the best. Only they reflected how the world really was.

In addition to this, Zhu Xi insisted that one needs a comprehensive understanding of the classics. Initially, in a given case, one's interpretation might well be mistaken, but Zhu believed that broad inquiry would eventually force one to abandon idiosyncratic views and be led toward the correct understanding. Zhu also urged students to debate among themselves in order to arrive at a better understanding. And, of course, students were also to consult with their teachers concerning their interpretations. In combination, this broadly based and multifaceted approach presents a powerful method of learning, but, as with all such proposals, it raises characteristic problems of its own. One such issue, which became a topic of debate among Neo-Confucians, is the tension between the need for both *bo* 博 "breadth" and *yue* 約 "a grasp of the essential."

Basically, the idea is that one needs to study extensively in order to appreciate fully the nuance and texture of a given moral principle. At the same time, throughout one's extensive study, one must be ever striving to discern and embrace the underlying and unifying principle at work. This second aspect of study is critical; without it, the work of learning becomes an endless gathering of unconnected facts. Wang Yangming was later to criticize Zhu Xi's approach as leading inevitably to such a fragmented, unproductive, and ultimately pointless accumulation of information. One can see how this might occur, and this criticism was no doubt an accurate description of some Neo-Confucians.

Wang insisted that any separation between *knowledge* and *action* (and Wang was speaking primarily about moral knowledge and action) would result in the pursuit of the former as an end unto itself. At its worst, the pursuit of knowledge, particularly knowledge of the classics, becomes a means for self-aggrandizement and personal profit. This was an acute problem for Chinese intellectuals of this time. For the path to official position and advancement required success in the imperial examinations, and mastery of the classics, which formed the core of the examinations, was indispensable for such success.

To respond to such criticism on Zhu's behalf, one might first point out that Zhu never advocated knowledge for knowledge's sake; he always united the tasks of *dao wenxue* "pursuing inquiry and study" and *zun dexing* "honoring the virtuous nature" with the attitude of *jing* "reverential attention." Study of the classics was never divorced from moral self cultivation. Moreover, it seems eminently reasonable to insist, as Zhu Xi does, that extensive study and lively debate is needed as a sort of proving ground for one's intuitions. Without some kind of pull toward objectivity it seems one can easily fall into a kind of solipsism. If one believes, as Zhu Xi did, that a proper understanding of a set of sacred texts is critical, if not necessary, for self cultivation, it seems wise to engage in philological and historical study, and to consider carefully what others have said and do say about the text. This kind of comprehensive, synthetic approach is well represented by Zhu Xi's own commentaries. For example, his commentaries on the *Four Books* is appropriately called "*Collected* Commentaries on the *Four Books*." It is not just Zhu Xi's personal musings on these texts; it is a collection of the philological, historical, textual, and interpretive efforts of many commentators throughout history, combined, synthesized, and augmented by Zhu's own views.

Zhu Xi believed that there was a single correct interpretation of the classics, that anyone who worked at them long enough, with dedicated effort and sincerity, would arrive at this same understanding, and that this proper understanding would transform the individual. In other words, the study of these texts was not just enriching or edifying, it was *enlightening*. That was the whole point of study. In order to grasp the full significance of these texts, one had to become a certain kind of person, and this required one to understand how the lessons contained in the classics applied in the actual world of daily human life. It also required one to maintain a certain calmness and purity of mind while engaged in this study. Though mastery of the Confucian canon was central to Zhu Xi's method of self cultivation, it was not an isolated pursuit. Alone, it would not result in moral enlightenment. However, he did seem to believe that for almost everyone it was the necessary starting point for self cultivation.

> With regard to the way of learning, nothing is more urgent than a
> thorough study of principles; and a thorough study of principles

must of necessity consist in book-learning. . . . As a result, the
words and the deeds [of the ancient sages] have all become
permanent and fundamental exemplars for later generations to
emulate. . . . These visible traces and necessary results are all
contained in the classics and histories. A person who wishes to
have a thorough knowledge of the principles in the world without
first seeking for them [in the classics and histories] is one who
wishes to go forward but ends up standing right in front of a wall.
This is why we say "a thorough study of principles must of
necessity consist in book-learning."[36]

Zhu Xi believed that textual study, properly pursued and augmented with
the other practices we have examined, eventually would result in a
comprehensive grasp of the truth. This is powerfully stated in his
commentary on the fifth chapter of the *Daxue*.

Once one has exerted effort in this way for a long time, there will
come a day when one achieves a wide and far-reaching penetration.
Then one will apprehend the internal and external, refined and
coarse qualities of all things, and one's mind, in its entirety and in
its every application will be perfectly clear.

When all is said and done, Zhu Xi relies on personal intuition to decide
when one has achieved such a state; however, it is an intuition which
comes only after extensive study, broad application, and careful reflection.
His method of moral self cultivation was a protracted process of refining
the self in order to recover the inherent *li* within. Wang Yangming will
argue that this is the right aim but the wrong approach. Wang insists that
we must concentrate on this inherent intuition, from the very start. If we
do not, we will never bring this capacity into full play. This initial
*discovery* is the most critical moment in the process of moral self
cultivation.

As was mentioned earlier, Zhu Xi's and Wang Yangming's
disagreement can be seen as a replaying of the argument between Xunzi
and Mengzi over whether thinking and reflection was the way of moral
self cultivation or whether one needed to acquire the moral sense through
learning. To state the disagreement in overly simple terms: if Xunzi and
Zhu Xi are correct, then becoming moral requires understanding and
transforming oneself in light of the wisdom of past sages. If Mengzi and
Wang are correct, then the sages and the classics at best may prove
helpful to the task of becoming moral, but they are not a necessary part of
moral self cultivation.[37] This tension, between the inherited wisdom of
the past and the original intuitions of contemporary individuals,
reemerges and courses throughout the Confucian tradition. It is visible

most often in debates between rival interpreters of the tradition over the proper means of self cultivation, though, as we have seen, this issue involves related concerns such as the true character of human nature. At different times, one side of this polarity rather than the other tended to be emphasized, though at no time was one pursued in complete isolation from the other. Like the notions of subjectivity and objectivity themselves, this proved to be an irreducible yet highly productive tension.[38]

# Notes

1. A number of recent studies on Zhu Xi's life and thought have greatly improved our understanding of him. Outstanding among these are: Wing-tsit Chan, ed., *Chu Hsi and Neo-Confucianism* (Honolulu, HI: University of Hawaii Press, 1986); Wing-tsit Chan, *Chu Hsi: New Studies* (Honolulu, HI: University of Hawaii Press, 1989); Daniel K. Gardner, *Learning to be a Sage* (Berkeley, CA: University of California Press, 1990); and Hoyt C. Tillman, *Confucian Discourse and Chu Hsi's Ascendency* (Honolulu, HI: University of Hawaii Press, 1992). For a remarkably insightful description of the rise of the distinctively Song dynasty milieu in which Zhu Xi worked, see Peter K. Bol, *"This Culture of Ours:" Intellectual Transitions in T'ang and Sung China* (Stanford, CA: Stanford University Press, 1992). While Bol does not address the influence of Buddhism on the thinkers of this period, he still captures the tenor of the *zeitgeist* and particularly how it differs from what came immediately before it.

2. A good summary of Zhu Xi's achievements is provided by Wing-tsit Chan in his *Chu Hsi: Life and Thought* (Hong Kong: The Chinese University Press, 1987). In particular, see "Chu Hsi's Completion of Neo-Confucianism," pp. 103-38.

3. In particular, his work on texts contributed to his influence on later generations. Zhu Xi was the first to group together the *Analects, Mengzi, Daxue,* and *Zhongyong* as the "Four Books." Since he completed this work, in 1190, these texts served as the focus of Confucian thought, and from 1313 until 1905, his commentaries on the four books provided the basis for the civil service examinations. Zhu Xi's extensive and elegant commentarial work provided a systematic, coherent, and powerful interpretation of the Confucian canon. This monumental textual work distinguished Zhu Xi from thinkers like Wang Yangming and secured the success of his school. For an important comparative study of commentarial traditions that throws considerable light on this aspect of Confucianism, see John B. Henderson, *Scripture, Canon, and Commentary: A Comparison of Confucian and Western Exegesis* (Princeton, NJ: Princeton University Press, 1991).

4. For example, see J. Percy Bruce, *Chu Hsi and His Masters* (London:

Probsthain, 1923) or Olaf Graf, *Tao und Jen: Sein und Sollen im sungchinesischen Monismus* (Wiesbaden: Harrassowitz, 1970).

5. For this reason alone, it is unfortunate that thinkers like Zhu Xi have come to be known in the west as "Neo-Confucians." They did not—as Neo-Platonists, Neo-Kantians, or Neo-Hegelians did—think of themselves as offering a *new and improved* version of Confucianism (though some did believe that they "filled-in" implicit lacunae in the tradition). They saw themselves as the legitimate inheritors and defenders of the one true tradition.

6. The most sophisticated study of the thought of Cheng Yi is by A. C. Graham, *Two Chinese Philosophers*, reprint (LaSalle, IL: Open Court, 1992). For an analysis of the general view of Cheng Yi and Zhu Xi, see his article, "What Was New in the Ch'eng-Chu Theory of Human Nature," in Chan, *Chu Hsi and Neo-Confucianism*, pp. 138-57. Note though that Graham—like many scholars who work on Neo-Confucianism—failed to appreciate the ways in which Buddhist thought influenced these later Confucians. For some of the ways this affects Graham's analysis, see Mark Berkson, Review of *Two Chinese Philosophers* in *Philosophy East and West* 45.2 (February, 1995): 292-7.

7. My account of Zhu Xi's thought, and Wang Yangming's as well, is predicated on the assumption that Neo-Confucians had developed a rich and complex metaphysical scheme that finds little precedent in early Confucian thought and that there is a close and critical relationship between this metaphysical scheme and their ethical philosophy. This point seems sadly underemphasized in contemporary scholarship. A notable and important exception is Thomas A. Metzger, *Escape from Predicament* (New York: Columbia University Press, 1977).

8. I realize that not all early Buddhists hold precisely the views I present here, but I believe that views like these are held by many representatives of the Buddhist position and that these views, or something very much like them, are fundamental to the Buddhist point of view. For an introduction to the Buddhist perspective, see Walpola Rahula, *What the Buddha Taught*, reprint (New York: Grove Press, 1974).

9. For a general introduction to Buddhism's arrival and transformation in China, see Kenneth Ch'en, *Buddhism in China: A Historical Survey* (Princeton, NJ: Princeton University Press, 1964). For a study of the interaction between Buddhism and indigenous Chinese traditions, see Arthur F. Wright, *Buddhism in Chinese History* (Stanford, CA: Stanford University Press, 1959). See also the monumental work by Heinrich Dumoulin, *Zen Buddhism: A History*, vol. 1 (New York: Macmillan Publishing Company, 1988): 63-297.

10. For philosophical accounts of "Buddha Nature," see Paul Williams, *Mahāyāna Buddhism: The Doctrinal Foundations* (London: Routledge, 1989): 96-115, and Sallie B. King, *Buddha Nature* (Albany, NY: SUNY Press, 1991).

11. See Phillip B. Yampolsky, *The Platform Sutra of the Sixth Patriarch* (New York: Columbia University Press, 1967): 128-44.

12. In texts like the *Platform Sutra*, we find the language shifting back and forth between claims that this obscuring dust is *unreal* and that it is *not part of our original nature*.

13. For an excellent general study of this idea, see Paul Demieville, "Le Miroir Spiritual," *Sinologica,* 1:2 (1947): 112-37. For a translation of this essay, see "The Mirror of the Mind" in Peter Gregory, ed., *Sudden and Gradual: Approaches to Enlightenment in Chinese Thought* (Honolulu, HI: University of Hawaii Press, 1987): 13-40.

14. See Burton Watson, tr., *The Complete Works of Chuang Tzu* (New York: Columbia University Press, 1968): 97. Cf. 142.

15. Zhu Xi's commentary on *Mengzi* 2A6 reads, in part, "*Duan* 'sprout' means *xu* 緒 'clue' or 'the end of a thread.' Because of the manifestation of these feelings, one can glimpse the original state of the nature. It's as if there were something hidden inside but one can see clues or indications of it on the outside." See *Sishu jizhu* 四書集注.

16. For a study of this term, see Wing-tsit Chan, "The Evolution of the Neo-Confucian Concept of *li* as Principle," *Tsing Hua Journal of Chinese Studies,* n.s. 4.2 (1964): 123-49. As helpful as this study is, it tends to underestimate the influence of Buddhism, especially the Huayan School (see n. 17). As we will see, the Neo-Confucian concept of *li* is much more than the earlier Daoist view of *li* as the grand design of the universe. It carries the added feature that the entirety of this design is present and discernible in every aspect of the universe.

17. This idea was often expressed through the metaphor of Indra's Net, an infinite net of jewels, each jewel reflecting all the others. This image appears in the *Treatise on the Golden Lion,* a famous and influential work of the Huayan School. For a translation, see Wm. Theodore de Bary, ed., *Sources of Chinese Tradition,* vol. 1 (New York: Columbia University Press, 1960): 329-33. For studies of the Huayan School of Buddhism, see Francis H. Cook, *Hua-yen Buddhism: The Jewel Net of Indra* (University Park, PA: Pennsylvania State University Press, 1977), Robert M. Gimello and Peter N. Gregory, eds., *Studies in Ch'an and Hua-yen* (Honolulu, HI: University of Hawaii Press, 1983) and Paul Williams, *Mahāyāna Buddhism: The Doctrinal Foundations,* pp. 116-38 .

18. Adapted from Wing-tsit Chan, *Source Book,* p. 623.

19. Earlier, we saw Mengzi rely upon this notion in his discussion of the "flood-like *qi*" (see p. 20). But by Zhu Xi's time, the meaning of this term had taken on complex metaphysical senses not fully visible and at times wholly foreign to its earlier cluster of meanings.

20. Cf. Chan, *Source Book,* p. 620.

21. I use the word *idea* with some trepidation since Neo-Confucians did not propose any kind of "picture" model.

22. Here and in what follows, Zhu Xi is referring to certain animal behavior, such as the "benevolence" wolves and tigers show to their young. Such phenomena serve as evidence for the universal presence of *li*. These creatures only partially manifest this particular *li* because the nature of their *qi* only allows a certain amount of it through. The *qi* of other creatures and things is so dense that none of this particular *li* is manifested. Many westerners are tempted, by passages like this, to equate *li* with Platonic Forms. This is a mistake. *Li* per se don't make a given thing the kind of thing it is. Actually, it is the fixed endowment of *qi* which makes a given thing the kind of thing it is. For *qi* determines which *li* get manifested.

23. Cf. Chan, *Source Book*, p. 621.

24. Zhu is invoking a well-known distinction first seen in the *History*, where we find the lines, "The human mind is precarious; the mind of the Way is subtle. . ." Cf. Legge, *The Shoo King*, p. 61.

25. Since the mind contains the principles of all things, once cultivated, it understands not only itself but the workings of all things. Thus Zhu Xi's theory of *li* and *qi* accomplishes many of the same philosophical goals as Plato's recollection theory. It enables him to explain the daunting problem of how we come to understand the world: the principles in our mind match up with the principles of the things out there in the world. This latter idea is retained in the modern Chinese word *lihui* 理會 "to understand." Literally it means *li* "principles" *hui* "meet," i.e., the principles within one's mind "meet" or "match up with" the principles of the phenomenon under investigation. Since we are endowed with the *li* at birth, Zhu Xi's theory, unlike Plato's, does not require a belief in reincarnation.

26. Zhu derives both these and the complementary set of special terms below from the twenty-seventh chapter of the *Zhongyong*. Here and throughout his work, the notions of the mind and the nature are more or less synonymous for Zhu Xi.

27. For a discussion of the role of meditation in Zhu Xi's thought, see Julia Ching, "Chu Hsi on Personal Cultivation," in Chan, ed., *Chu Hsi and Neo-Confucianism*, pp. 282-4. The distinctions I draw between "preserving the mind" and "pursuing inquiry and study" and the mediating attitude of "reverential attention" were seen by Zhu Xi as aspects of a single task. One cannot help but see them as Confucian correlates to the Chan practices of *ding* 定 "meditative calm," *hui* 慧 "insight," and *yixingsanmei* 一行三昧 "mindful practice," respectively. As texts like the *Platform Sutra* make clear, these too are but aspects of a single task.

28. Zhu Xi did not have a set method for how to carry out "quiet sitting." It was not a developed technique of meditation with specific postures and practices designed to bring one to specific states of consciousness. It was

more a period of dedicated calm in which one was to reflect upon and restore oneself.

29. Different Confucian thinkers understood this term in distinct and different ways. For a brief discussion and comparison of its different senses, see my *Ethics in the Confucian Tradition: The Thought of Mencius and Wang Yang-ming*, pp. 81, 107-8. See also D. C. Lau, "A Note on *ko-wu*," *Bulletin of the School of Oriental and African Studies*, 30 (1967): 535-37.

30. This is the same character that was used in early Chinese discussions of the need for the king to "revere" his virtue. See the Introduction, pp. x- xi.

31. It is important to realize, though, that earlier Confucians appealed to a much more limited set of canonical texts. The notion of a "classical text" was not explicitly described until the time of Xunzi.

32. As was noted earlier, Zhu Xi was the first to assemble these texts into a set. It should also be noted that *none* of these texts, with the possible exception of the *Analects,* was studied by any of the earlier Confucians we have discussed. And, of course, it was not studied by Kongzi or his immediate disciples.

33. Chan, *Source Book*, pp. 85-6.

34. Sima Guang 司馬光 (1019-1086) was the first to treat the text as an independent work. For a brief but illuminating discussion of its history, see Chan, *Source Book*, p. 85 note 5.

35. This rather loose designation refers to those associated with the thought of Lu Xiangshan 陸象山 (1139-1193 C.E.) and Wang Yangming. This group is opposed to the Cheng-Zhu School, those associated with the thought of Cheng Yi and Zhu Xi. For a study of Lu Xiangshan's thought, see Huang Siu-chi, *Lu Hsiang-shan: A Twelfth Century Chinese Idealist Philosopher*, reprint (Westport, CT: Hyperion Press, 1977).

36. The translation is by Yü Ying-shih. See his "Morality and Knowledge in Chu Hsi's Philosophical System," in Wing-tsit Chan, ed., *Chu Hsi and Neo-Confucianism,* p. 233. Yü discusses the issue of the role of book-learning on pages 233-5 and 245-7.

37. This is overly simple because Zhu Xi's and Wang Yangming's profoundly different assumptions about human nature and very different metaphysical beliefs complicate any such comparison. However, as to the method of self cultivation, such a generalization holds true and is revealing.

38. Though he does not state it quite this way, I take this to be at least consistent with a theme that runs throughout the early work of Thomas Nagel. It informs many of the essays in his classic work *Mortal Questions* (London: Cambridge University Press, 1979). See especially the essay entitled "Subjective and Objective," pp. 196-213.

# 王陽明

# 5. Wang Yangming

It is, of course, impossible to give an adequate picture of *any* person's life and thought in the span of a single chapter. In the case of Wang Yangming (1472-1529 C.E.),[1] one feels this difficulty even more acutely, for he seems to have lived not just one but several lives. He was a scholar, a poet, a renowned calligrapher, a successful provincial governor, a triumphant general, and the most influential and charismatic moral teacher of his day.[2] I will concentrate on this last aspect of his life, and, in keeping with the theme of the present study, will focus my attention primarily upon his method of self cultivation.

Like Zhu Xi, Wang saw himself as the inheritor and defender—against enemies both within and without—of Confucianism. In particular, he saw himself as the true disciple and defender of Mengzi, the fourth-century B.C.E. Confucian whose thought we explored in chapter two. I have argued that Mengzi taught a *development model* of moral self cultivation in which people, through practice and reflection upon their innate and fragile moral sense, could develop and extend these "moral sprouts," until they became strong and vital moral dispositions.

In the previous chapter, I also argued that profound changes had occured in the Confucian intellectual paradigm in the course of the nearly fifteen hundred years separating thinkers like Zhu Xi from Mengzi, and I sought to explain briefly some of those changes that most affected the issues surrounding moral self cultivation. By Wang's time this major shift in Confucian moral thinking had been in place for several hundred years. As noted earlier, the sources of this shift can be traced to the rise and reign of Daoist and Buddhist thought that began around the first century C.E. and only began to subside around the ninth century.[3] Though the tide of Daoist and Buddhist thought began to ebb, its influence remained, and the course of Chinese philosophy had changed dramatically under this influence.

One result of the broad and complex interaction of Daoism, Buddhism, and Confucianism was a profound shift away from Mengzi's *development model* of moral self cultivation, which was grounded in his distinctive theory of human nature, to theories that were based on comprehensive metaphysical theories about the world. We saw a clear manifestation of this shift in Zhu Xi's thought and it is a distinctive feature of every Neo-Confucian thinker. Mengzi's ethical theory was grounded in assumptions about moral psychology and a philosophical anthropology, i.e., theories about what kinds of creatures human beings are and how they act as social creatures. By Zhu's and Wang's time, ethical theories were grounded in views about universal moral principles, lying unnoticed or obscured beneath the hustle and bustle of day-to-day activities. These theories now provided the warrants for how one should organize and live one's life. Mengzi's theory that we all possess moral sprouts, a young and fragile moral sense that requires concerted and prolonged effort to nurture to maturity and refinement, had become a belief in an innate and fully formed *moral mind*: a complete and perfect moral guide that was buried beneath our selfish desires.

One can see this philosophical difference manifested in a dramatic shift in metaphors. Wang did not talk about "sprouts" or employ Mengzi's panoply of agricultural images. He spoke of the moral mind as *the sun shining behind clouds* and *a clear, bright mirror hidden beneath dust*. Our moral sensibilities were fully formed and quite formidable *faculties* that were obscured by the "clouds" and "dust" of selfish desires.[4] These are images Mengzi never used and this is not only because they are borrowed from Buddhist texts which he had not seen, they reflect a set of assumptions about the nature of human beings and the universe which he did not share or ever entertain.

This had profound effects on both the possibilities for and conceptions of the process of moral self cultivation. It led to what I refer to as *recovery* or *discovery models* of moral self cultivation.[5] These new models of self cultivation opened up exciting and attractive new possibilities. For example, Wang and other later Confucians could and did talk about the experience of dramatic and complete moral *enlightenment*.[6] Given their views, it became possible to awaken to complete and perfect moral knowledge; one could *discover* and bring fully into play one's innate moral mind. Some believed this goal could be reached with a single moment of sincere effort; indeed Wang believed such an effort constituted proper practice. These kinds of ideas are completely foreign to Mengzi; it simply is impossible to *develop* like this. While Zhu Xi holds his own unique version of these views, in Wang they assume a distinct and dramatic form.

While Mengzi advocated the persistent and careful cultivation of one's moral sprouts and Xunzi urged us to acquire a second, moral nature through persistent study and practice, later Confucians increasingly concentrated, sometimes exclusively, on the elimination of one's *selfish desires*. These later Confucians exhibit a passionate and at times frenetic preoccupation with the goal of moral enlightenment and with the challenge of maintaining unceasing, internal vigilance over their each and every thought. Their aim is to develop and sustain a state of mind in which they constantly monitor themselves for the slightest trace of selfishness. For them, moral self cultivation comes to resemble the tasks of relieving oneself of and guarding against self-deception. Since one already possesses a complete and perfect moral mind, the challenge is to identify it, engage it, and preserve it from obscuration. The source of obscuration also lies within the self—misguided applications of the mind that generate selfish desires. Wang's teachings purport to offer a unique form of *moral therapy,* designed to address this pernicious form of self-deception.

I will explore three distinctive aspects of Wang's general theory of moral self cultivation. The first of these, *the unity of knowledge and action,* is Wang's most well known teaching and was mentioned briefly in my discussion of Zhu Xi's method of self cultivation above.[7] The question of the relationship between moral knowledge and action is an idea with a very old pedigree in China (and elsewhere as well). Wang's particular version of it has had a profound influence on later East Asian thought and culture.[8] It still exerts great influence and retains strong appeal. For example, in one of Yukio Mishima's great novels, *Runaway Horses,* Wang's teaching is ardently embraced by the central figure, Isao.[9] It culminates in his assassination of a powerful member of a *zaibatsu* ("corporate conglomerate") which Isao and others believe is undermining their society. Isao's *knowledge* of the malignant nature of the *zaibatsu* precipitated his *action.* As Wang argued, such knowledge is the beginning of action and such action the completion of knowledge.

While the nature of the relationship between moral knowledge and action involves familiar problems about issues like the reason-giving force of moral propositions, claims about a *unity* of knowledge and action might strike one as a bit strange at first, for it seems that we often *know* we should (or should not) act in a certain way and yet we fail to act accordingly. Wang would simply deny this, but we have to understand much more about how he saw things in order to appreciate *why* he would hold such a view and what such a denial entails.

The problem of the relationship between moral knowledge and action is not unique to China, nor is China the only place where we find disagreement over how to address this issue. At first glance, Socrates seems to say something very similar to Wang; he believed that we could never act against knowledge. If we *knew* the good we would *do* the good, and if someone did not do the right thing, it must be the case that this person simply lacked complete knowledge of the good.[10] However, as we shall see, Socrates' view ends up being significantly different from Wang's. Socrates had an intellectualist view of moral action; he didn't fully appreciate how appetites, passions, and desires often interfere with our rational knowledge of what is right and prevent us from acting appropriately. In his own unique fashion, Wang was very concerned with just these aspects of human behavior and much of his philosophy concerns how to manage these various aspects of the self. In addition, Wang believed that moral knowledge brought forth new and needed desires and affections; whereas, on the Socratic model, knowledge could at best redirect our inherent desires, appetites, and passions.

Given his understanding of things, Socrates did not have an adequate way to account for or accommodate problems like *weakness of will*. Later thinkers in the early Greek and western tradition developed more elaborate pictures of moral psychology in which different parts of the self could be in conflict with one another.[11] They also developed views of the self in which our different parts could influence and shape one another.[12] In time, the idea of a distinct mental power, the *will*, was introduced, as a way of bridging the gap that one often finds looming between the course of action we know we should take and what we actually do.[13] Of course, the notion of will, while answering certain vexing questions concerning the phenomenon of moral failure, generates special difficulties of its own. In particular, as a moral teacher, it leaves one in a difficult bind. For, when someone claims she *knows* what is right to do yet finds that she cannot act in accordance with her knowledge, if you are convinced that she does in fact know, all that seems to be left to do is to insist that she *just do it!* But what is a teacher to do if, as is often the case, the student insists, "I'm trying as hard as I can but find that I still can't do it!"?

This admittedly brief and selective survey of issues prepares the ground for our discussion of Wang's view of *the unity of knowledge and action*. Wang did not approach the problem of moral failure—cases where one knows one should act in a certain way but fails to so act—in terms of a Socratic lack of knowledge or Augustinian weakness of will. He had a different set of philosophical tools with which to work; prominent among them was a distinction between *zhenzhi* 眞知 "real knowledge" and *changzhi* 常知 "ordinary knowledge."[14] Later Confucians believed that there was a significant difference between *knowledge about* something and *knowledge of* something. The former kind of knowledge is "ordinary" in the sense that it is commonplace, most everyone has it. The latter kind of knowledge is "real" in that it arises out of personal experience and brings together both cognitive and affective types of knowing. This distinction is not universally applicable. For example, it doesn't apply to imaginary objects, like unicorns, which no one has *knowledge of*. But it may remain meaningful even in cases of highly abstract knowledge, such as mathematical knowledge; there is a significant difference between knowing about a given geometric proof and grasping its significance in the way a great mathematician does.[15] But Wang and his fellow Confucians were not much interested in these kinds of cases; they were primarily interested in moral knowledge and in this regard the distinction between "real" and "ordinary" knowledge does some major work.

Perhaps the easiest way to understand and appreciate the distinction between *real* and *ordinary* knowledge is to follow the Confucian practice of explaining things by means of parable. Cheng Yi[16] captured the distinction between these two types of knowledge in a memorable way and used it to describe the relationship between moral knowledge and action. He said:

> *Real knowledge* is different from *ordinary knowledge*. I was once with a farmer who had been mauled by a tiger, when someone happened to mention that a tiger was mauling people in the area. [Naturally], everyone was alarmed. But this one farmer had on his face an expression that differed from the rest. Everyone, even a child, knows tigers maul people, but they do not possess *real knowledge*. It is only *real knowledge* if it is like that of the farmer. When people continue to do what they know they should not do, this is because they do not *really know* it is wrong. If they *really knew*, they would not do it.[17]

*Real knowledge* embraces both proper cognitive and affective aspects. In cases requiring moral action, one not only knows what to do but finds oneself properly motivated to do so. In genuine cases of real knowledge, an agent simply spontaneously moves toward the proper end. Those who possess such knowledge cannot but act in accordance with it; this is what separates them from most of us, who possess only ordinary knowledge. *Real knowledge* is self-activating in the same way that genuine virtues are; when faced with situations of a certain kind, a person with *real knowledge* will simply respond in an appropriate manner. There is no need to perceive, select, judge, and will; this is to have three acts too many. The perfected person responds like a mirror, accurately and immediately "reflecting" the situation at hand.[18]

On one occasion, Wang sets forth his views on this issue while answering one of his disciples. The disciple said:

> "Now there are people who, despite knowing they should be filial to their parents and respectful to their elder brother, cannot be filial or respectful. From this it is clear that knowledge and action are two separate things."
>
> [Wang replied, "In this case, knowledge and action] have already been separated by selfish desires; this is not the original state of knowledge and action. There have never been people who know but do not act. Those who know but do not act, simply do not yet know. . . . Thus the *Daxue* ("Great Learning") gives us examples of *real knowledge and action,* saying it is 'like loving a beautiful color or hating a bad odor.'"[19]

As mentioned earlier, Wang believed we all possess an innate, perfect, and fully formed moral mind which, in some deep sense, always knows what we ought to do. But selfish desires interfere with the operation of this innate moral mind, our ever-present moral conscience, obscuring its effectiveness and bringing about the "separation" of knowledge and action. As Wang goes on to explain in the same passage,

> It is like a person with a stuffed-up nose. Even if he sees a malodorous object before him, he does not smell it, and so he does not hate it. This is simply not to know the odor. This is just like the case of saying someone [who does not act appropriately] knows filial piety or brotherly respect. That person must have already acted with filial piety or brotherly respect before he can be said to know them. One cannot say he knows filial piety or brotherly respect, simply because he knows how to say something filial or brotherly.

From his theoretical claim about the unity of knowledge and action, Wang draws the practical conclusion that one cannot possess *real knowledge* until one has actually acted in the appropriate way. For Wang, you cannot know what courage is until you have acted courageously and you cannot really understand what compassion is until you have acted compassionately. Someone who really "knows" courage or compassion will spontaneously act in a courageous or compassionate manner, whenever these are called for.

It should seem a bit odd that Wang considers the cases of hating a bad odor and loving a beautiful color as *actions*. We tend to regard these as *affections*—not *actions*.[20] However, Wang would insist that they are part of a continuum of *knowing, feeling, intending,* and *acting*. He expresses this organic unity of knowing and acting with the formula "Knowledge is the beginning of action and action the completion of knowledge."[21] Wang sees the problem of moral failure and the solution to the problem very differently from either Socrates or Augustine. For Socrates, the person who fails to act morally simply needs to know more. For Augustine, she needs to engage in an act of will. But for Wang, such a person needs to *become sincere,* i.e., be true to her innate moral mind. One accomplishes this by eliminating the obscuring influences of one's selfish thoughts.[22]

One often gets the impression that Wang saw himself as a spiritual *therapist* rather than a philosophical *theorist*. His primary concern was getting people moving in the right direction. A number of aspects of his philosophical position appear at best problematic and others are left rather vague. But in teaching individual students he is always clear, direct, and to the point. Often one can feel the power of his personality and the energy of his exchanges with students. It is clear that a great deal was at stake in these meetings and conversations. However, it is equally clear that much of what Wang accomplished was more the result of his inspiring presence and dramatic delivery than it was a consequence of the cogency of his arguments.[23]

Let us now turn to another aspect of Wang's theory of moral self cultivation and discuss what he thought we needed to do in order to become sincere. According to Wang, people deluded themselves and, in the process, lost sight of their innate moral mind. He believed the causes of this unfortunate phenomenon were numerous, but we shall restrict our attention to one cause which he seemed to find particularly bothersome, perhaps because it concerned a mistake in how to pursue self cultivation itself. This problem can best be described as the overintellectualization of the task of self cultivation.

Wang believed that in order for self cultivation to work, it had to directly concern the actual activities of one's own life. For example, one of Wang's disciples, who was an official, complained that he had inadequate time for self cultivation because he was so busy listening to litigation.[24] Wang jumped on this opportunity to make two related points to this disciple. First, he told him that he had ample opportunity to engage in self cultivation, for whenever he was listening to legal cases he could examine himself to see whether he was being perfectly sincere. During these times, he should guard against the intrusion of even the slightest selfish thought which would interfere with his performance as a fair and good judge. Second, this kind of opportunity is his only *real* opportunity for moral improvement. What he took to be moral self cultivation—studying some classic or engaging in meditation—isn't the best kind of self cultivation at all. At best, such pursuits might help him to avoid going further astray, but they will never help him advance. More likely, they will interfere with his moral growth, for he will come to regard them as ends unto themselves. This not only distracts attention from the true work of self cultivation—which must take place in the arena of one's own life—but over time, it will lead him to begin competing with others over who knows more about the classics, or he will mistake meditative calm as the goal and drift into quietism.

Wang described this aspect of his teachings in terms of a passage from the *Mengzi*, in which Mengzi talked about the need to continually work on the task of self cultivation. Wang understood a line from this passage in his own particular way. Mengzi had said, *biyou shiyan* 必有 事焉 "always work at self cultivation." [25] Wang took this to mean, "[in self cultivation] always work on *your own personal problems*." That is to say, if you don't have your own problem to work on, self cultivation simply won't work. In fact, such effort often has extremely negative results. It can lead one away from genuine moral engagement and result in a profound alienation from morality and an obsession with selfish pursuits. Trying to improve oneself morally, in the absence of some actual, personal moral problem was, according to Wang:

> just like cooking rice by heating a pot. If one does not put in water and rice, and only concentrates on adding fuel and starting the fire, I don't know what kind of thing you will cook up. I am afraid the pot will crack before the fire can be properly adjusted.[26]

Wang's point here can be understood in terms of the earlier discussion between ordinary and real knowledge. One will never attain real knowledge of morality unless one works on real problems. And the only real problems—those that engage one's heart and challenge one to become aware of and work to eliminate the selfishness that stands in the way of moral imporvement—are those that one confronts (or avoids) every day, in one's own life.

If I were to apply Wang's teaching to my own life, which of course he would insist I do if my goal is real knowledge, I would see many reasons for concern and only some for hope. This in itself might be seen as progress, since it generates some sense of my need for and the demanding nature of moral improvement. Since I am interested in ethics, Wang would want me to be careful not to confuse *knowing about* ethical philosophy with *being* a better person. While few philosophers would confuse these two (and none should), we do tend to believe—perhaps wrongly or at least too strongly—that a *theoretical* understanding of ethical issues plays a central role in becoming a better person. Instead, Wang emphasized the need to cultivate certain affective states and saw these as playing a critical *cognitive role* in moral understanding.[27] Wang would also warn me not to become obsessed with my interest in ethical philosophy or even my desire to become moral, for these too can become impediments to moral well-being. Either of these might lead me to ignore or even trample over family, friends, students, and colleagues in order, on one hand, to win professional success and recognition, or, on the other, to pursue a grim and lonely conception of moral improvement.

On the positive side, if I take up and follow Wang's advice, I will see that I have ample—practically speaking, unlimited—opportunities for moral self cultivation. For the proper objects of my moral attention are the actual affairs of my everyday life. I don't need to wait for dramatic opportunities that require moral courage, compassion, and wisdom of heroic proportions. Quite the contrary, I should concentrate on more modest moral challenges. I should work on monitoring and correcting my behavior as a son, husband, teacher, colleague, friend, etc. These areas of life present me with *real* moral problems, real in the sense that working through them will have efficacious results on my own moral progress. Here again we clearly see the therapeutic orientation of Wang's thought.

I have described Wang's ideal method of self cultivation as, in at least one respect, more "modest." But it is important to realize that, taken as a whole, it is rather demanding; he insisted on uninterrupted self-scrutiny. He wanted us to maintain constant inner scrutiny of every thought and be ever-vigilant against the intrusion of selfishness. If we could sustain this state of uninterrupted inner vigilance, our innate moral minds would recognize each and every selfish thought as it arose. Such awareness in itself had the power to eliminate the selfishness, provided of course that our self-knowledge was sincere.[28] Wang describes this state in a dramatic and most memorable passage:

> This effort must be carried out continuously. Like eradicating robbers and thieves, one must resolve to wipe them out completely. In idle moments one must search out and discover each and every selfish thought for sex, wealth, fame and the rest. One must resolve to pluck out and cast away the root of the sickness, so that it can never arise again. Only then may one begin to feel at ease. One must, at all times, be like a cat catching mice—with eyes intently watching and ears intently listening. As soon as a single [selfish] thought begins to stir, one must conquer it and cast it out. Act as if you were cutting a nail in two or slicing through iron. Do not indulge or accommodate it in any way. Do not harbor it, and do not allow it to escape.[29]

I would like to explore one final aspect of Wang's views on self cultivation, which I will call the *existential flavor* of his teachings. Wang's beliefs about an innate moral mind and the need to pursue self cultivation in the affairs of one's own life led him to see moral choice as extremely context-sensitive, and the moral life as an intensely personal and rather isolated affair. We can understand these aspects of his thinking as results of his desire to reorient people to the critical importance of personal commitment in pursuit of the moral life, but it led Wang to be an extremely iconoclastic Confucian and gave his teachings what I am calling a kind of *existential flavor*.[30]

For example, one of Wang's earliest disciples, his brother-in-law Xu Ai, in a preface to the work now known as the 傳習錄 *Chuanxilu*, tells us that one day Wang noticed a student recording his instructions.[31] Wang admonished this disciple saying that he taught in the same way a doctor prescribes medicine, he diagnoses the problem with each student on a case-by-case basis, supplies and adjusts the dosage of the appropriate medicine, and in this way *cures* each student's spiritual malady. If someone writes down these prescriptions and starts passing them out to people on the street, he will not only not help them, he will probably cause them great harm!

Of course, the student, and all his fellow students as well, immediately stopped writing down Wang's teachings. However, a short time later, the student who had been admonished by Wang discovered Xu Ai making a record of what the master had said. He immediately upbraided Xu Ai by repeating the words of the master. Xu calmly responded that he remembered the master's words well enough, and that unfortunately it seemed as if only *he* had truly understood them. For, as Xu Ai went on to explain, Wang's warning to not record his teachings was itself a prescription for a given ailment, a teaching tailored to a specific occasion and individual; it did not apply *now*, to Xu Ai.

This example illustrates the highly context-sensitive nature of moral judgment and the intensely personal character of moral decision in Wang's school. In Wang and his disciples we see a true religious faith in the power of the innate moral mind; they regarded it as a faculty, akin to seeing or hearing, that allowed them to realize what is right in each and every situation they encountered. If one could keep selfish thoughts from clouding the moral mirror of one's innate mind, it would spontaneously and accurately "reflect" the true dimensions and precise features of every situation that came before it. Borrowing a term from the *Mengzi,* Wang referred to this innate moral faculty as *liangzhi* 良知 "pure knowing."³² One of his poems well represents his faith in the power of this inner light.

> The thousand sages are all passing shadows;
> *liangzhi* alone is my teacher.³³

For Wang, one should always steer by one's own inner light; first, because each moral choice is original and unique, and, second, because only such choices provide one with genuine opportunities for moral self cultivation. Such views led him, among other things, to a less reverential attitude toward the Confucian tradition. He once said:

> In learning, the important thing is to get it with the mind. Even words from the mouth of Kongzi, if one seeks in one's mind and finds them to be wrong, dare not be accepted as true. . . . Even words from the mouth of an ordinary person, if one seeks in one's mind and finds them to be correct, dare not be regarded as false.³⁴

Wang went so far as to imply that we would be better off without the Confucian classics themselves, since at best these are records of past examples of the moral mind at work. At one point, he even condones the infamous "burning of the books" by the notorious first emperor of the

Qin dynasty.[35] According to Wang, we cannot improve ourselves by mimicking the classics, for *our* task is here, at hand, in our own lives. The classics and the sages themselves had no clear role to play in Wang's conception of the Confucian tradition. They cannot offer one *real knowledge* and pose potential threats to genuine practice.

The individuality of moral self cultivation led Wang to present the moral life as one which often led to a kind of righteous isolation.[36] Wang's followers had an awesome moral duty that compelled them to act in ways that most people simply could not understand. He once described this situation:

> There have been times when a man sees his father, son or brother falling into a deep ravine and drowning. He cries out and goes crawling, half-dressed and barefoot, stumbling and falling [in a mad dash] to save them. He dangles from dangerous cliffs and precipices in order to reach them. Looking on are some "proper gentlemen," who chattering and laughing amongst themselves and ceremoniously bowing to one another, consider the man to be insane, for so discarding proper etiquette—stripping off his clothes, crying out, stumbling and falling like this. . . . But [this man] pays no mind even to the danger of drowning, much less is he concerned about being ridiculed as insane! . . . There is nothing wrong with people saying that I am insane. The minds of all people throughout the world are the same as my mind. While there still are people who are insane—how can I not be so? While there still are people who have lost their minds—how can I not lose mine.[37]

In Wang, we see a radical version of Mengzi's moral intuitionism and a unique expression of the Confucian vision. Though iconoclastic in many ways, Wang himself was a consummate Confucian gentleman, a dedicated official, and a tireless moral teacher. His commitment to the moral life and his belief that this life consists of the cultivation of the self and the improvement of society, with the ultimate goal being the perfection of both, reveals him to be an original and worthy member of Kongzi's lineage.

# *Notes*

1. Tu Wei-ming has written an interesting work on Wang's early life, a Neo-Confucian version of Erik Erikson's *Young Man Luther.* See his *Neo-Confucian Thought in Action: Wang Yang-ming's Youth (1472-1509)* (Berkeley, CA: University of California Press, 1976). Julia Ching's study of Wang's spiritual quest is also most valuable. See *To Acquire Wisdom: The Way of Wang Yang-ming* (New York: Columbia University Press, 1976).

Wing-tsit Chan has produced the most important translation of Wang's teachings. See his *Instructions for Practical Living and Other Neo-Confucian Writings by Wang Yang-ming* (New York: Columbia University Press, 1963). Julia Ching's translation of Wang's philosophical letters is also an important source. See *The Philosophical Letters of Wang Yang-ming* (Columbia, SC: University of South Carolina Press, 1973). My *Ethics in the Confucian Tradition* compares aspects of Wang's ethical philosophy to aspects in Mengzi's thought and argues that Wang represents a distinct and quite radical form of the Mengzian vision.

2. Chang Yü-ch'üan wrote a most helpful series of articles on Wang's political and military accomplishments. See his "Wang Shou-jen as a Statesman," *Chinese Social and Political Science Review*, 23: 30-99, 155-7, 319-75, 473-517. A reprint of these articles is now available: (Arlington, VA: University Publications of America, 1975).

3. This is not to say that Daoism and Buddhism did not continue to be influential or develop after this point in Chinese history. However, Confucianism regained considerable strength and influence beginning around this time and there was a true renaissance of Confucian thinking.

4. For Wang's use of the sun and clouds imagery, see Chan, *Instructions*, sections 21, 62, 76, 167, and 171. For the mirror and dust imagery, see sections 207, 237, 255, 289, and 290. This of course only gives us examples from one record of Wang's teachings; these are not the only examples nor the only metaphors he uses to convey his view of things.

5. I use the former to refer to Zhu Xi's view and the latter to Wang Yangming's. While these two models share many similar assumptions, they tend to diverge over the issues of how accessible moral knowledge is and what is the necessary or best way to engage this knowledge and get it to inform one's perceptions, judgments, and actions.

6. Wang uses the character *wu* 悟 "enlightenment" (familiar to many in the west by its Japanese pronounciation, "satori") some thirty times in the course of the major collection of his teachings, the *Chuanxilu*. This character and this general way of talking about moral development are not found anywhere in the *Mengzi*. The idea that some people are able to attain an immediate understanding of the true nature of the mind and that this itself is true practice can be seen most clearly in the famous "Teaching in Four Axioms" (Chan, section 315). This conversation, between Wang and his two most advanced students, finds a clear parallel in chapter 16 of the *Platform Sutra*.

7. See p. 51.

8. Perhaps the earliest explicit reference to this problem is found in the *History*, where a minister named Fu Yue declares to his king that, "It is not knowing that is difficult but acting." See James Legge, tr., *The Chinese Classics, Vol. 3, The Shoo King*, reprint (Hong Kong: Hong Kong University Press, 1970): 258. For a study of the history of this idea from

Wang Yangming to Mao Zedong, see David S. Nivison, "The Problem of 'Knowledge' and 'Action' in Chinese Thought Since Wang Yang-ming," in Arthur F. Wright, ed., *Studies in Chinese Thought* (Chicago: University of Chicago Press, 1953): 112-45.

9. See Michael Gallagher, tr., *Runaway Horses* (New York: Pocket Books, 1975): 353-4.

10. Socrates purportedly put forth this view in the *Protagoras* (349e-361c). See W. K. C. Guthrie, tr. (London: Penguin Books, 1979).

11. For example, in Book IV of the *Republic* (412b-427c), Plato introduces a tripartite picture of the soul in which the passionate and appetitive parts vie with our desire for the good, which is associated with the rational part of the soul. See the *Republic*, G. M. A. Grube, tr., C. D. C. Reeve, rev. (Indianapolis, IN: Hackett Publishing Company, 1992).

12. Aristotle presents his view of the intellect's ability to shape the passions and appetites through habituation to the good in the *Nicomachean Ethics* (1103a15-1103b25 and 1144b1-1145a5). See Terence Irwin, tr., (Indianapolis, IN: Hackett Publishing Company, 1985). For an extremely helpful study of Aristotle's view of moral learning, see M. F. Burnyeat, "Aristotle on Learning to be Good," in Amélie Oksenberg Rorty, *Essays on Aristotle's Ethics* (Berkeley, CA: University of California Press, 1980): 69-92. For an essay that focuses on the executive role that the intellect plays in this process, see Richard Sorabji, "Aristotle on the Role of the Intellect in Virtue," in the same volume, pp. 201-19.

13. In *The Theory of Will in Classical Antiquity*, Albrecht Dihle argues that Augustine is the first to articulate a distinct mental power, *voluntas* ("will"), which directs and orders human desires and that this discovery arose out of his personal struggle as described in the *Confessions*.

14. For a discussion of the early development of this distinction, see my *Ethics in the Confucian Tradition: The Thought of Mencius and Wang Yang-ming*, pp. 66-7.

15. Wang's distinction in some ways resembles Gilbet Ryle's distinction between "knowing that" and "knowing how." People can know that dribbling a basketball entails handling it in a certain specific way and yet may be wholly incapable of so handling it. They know what dribbling is but lack the know-how to do it. See Gilbert Ryle, *The Concept of Mind* (London: Hutchinson's University Library, 1949): 25-61.

16. See p. 43.

17. *Henan Chengshi yishu*, 2A:2b-3a (*SBBY*).

18. This is Wang's way of talking, and it conveys his view of things very well. However, the mirror metaphor breaks down at a certain point: for mirrors do not *act*, whereas the sage surely does. Cf. pp. 45-6.

19. Adapted from Chan, *Instructions*, section 5.

20. This point was first made by David S. Nivison. See his "Review of *Instructions for Practical Living and Other Neo-Confucian Writings by Wang Yang-ming* by Wing-tsit Chan and *Instructions for Practical Life* by Goodrich Henke," *Journal of the American Oriental Society*, 84.4 (1964): 437.

21. See Chan, *Instructions*, section 5. Wang also uses the formula, "Knowledge and action advance together." See sections 133, 136.

22. I follow the standard practice of translating the Chinese character *cheng* 誠 as "sincere" with the qualification that this means "true to one's innate moral mind." A. C. Graham sought to bring out this sense of the word by translating it as "integrity." See his *Two Chinese Philosophers*. The idea is that a thing is *cheng* when it is as it ought to be, i.e., when it follows its *li*. And so being sincere for Wang means realizing or bringing into being the true state of one's nature. This is appropriately thought of as "integrity."

23. In some respects, Wang was a kind of spiritual coach, but he was also a kind of *guru* figure to his disciples. For an interesting study that explores the various facets of Wang as a religious teacher by applying insights borrowed from Kierkegaard, see Lee H. Yearley, "Teachers and Saviors," *The Journal of Religion*, 65.2 (April, 1985): 225-43.

24. For this passage, see Chan, *Instructions*, section 218. Cf. 137 and 294. In the latter passage, we find Wang himself listening to and resolving a difficult legal case in a most ingenious manner.

25. For a more complete discussion of this aspect of Wang's teaching, see my *Ethics in the Confucian Tradition: The Thought of Mencius and Wang Yang-ming*, pp. 83-4, 89-90.

26. See my *Ethics in the Confucian Tradition: The Thought of Mencius and Wang Yang-ming*, p. 84. Cf. Chan, *Instructions*, section 186.

27. One's affective state can play a critical role in how one perceives a given situation. For example, when a totally heartless person, walking home on a winter's night, comes upon a shivering homeless person blocking his path, all he might see is an obstacle to his progress. Such a deficiency proved tragic for King Lear: "[He] that will not see, because he does not feel" (*King Lear*, 4.1, 70-1). See Kenneth Muir, ed. (London: Methuen and Company Ltd. 1952): 151. I owe the reference to Bryan W. Van Norden.

28. See Chan, *Instructions*, sections 241, 290.

29. See my *Ethics in the Confucian Tradition: The Thought of Mencius and Wang Yang-ming*, p. 85. Cf. Chan, *Instructions*, section 39.

30. Okada Takehiko sees Wang's thought as strongly existential. See his "Wang Chi and the Rise of Existentialism," in Wm. Theodore de Bary, ed., *Self and Society in Ming Thought* (New York: Columbia University Press, 1970): 121-44. David S. Nivison offers some important qualifications to such a view. See his "Moral Decision in Wang Yang-ming: The Problem of

Chinese 'existentialism'," *Philosophy East and West*, 23.1-2 (1973): 121-38. I have explored this issue in more depth in an article discussing these two early treatments. See "Existentialism in the School of Wang Yangming" in Philip J. Ivanhoe, ed., *Chinese Language, Thought, and Culture*, (LaSalle, IL: Open Court Press, 1996): 250-64. See also Nivison's response on pp. 336-41 of the same volume.

31. The *Chuanxilu* is the work translated by Chan and Henke. A translation of the preface can be found in Appendix I of my *Ethics in the Confucian Tradition: The Thought of Mencius and Wang Yang-ming*, pp. 115-16.

32. The term occurs only once, in 7A15, and there lacks the special sense it has in Wang's use. Roughly speaking, for Mengzi it described a nascent capacity while for Wang it described an innate faculty.

33. *Wang Wenchenggong quanshu*, 20.632b (*SBCK*).

34. Chan, *Instructions*, section 173.

35. For this reference and a general discussion of Wang's attitude toward the classics, see my *Ethics in the Confucian Tradition: The Thought of Mencius and Wang Yang-ming*, pp. 102-112. For an account of the burning of the books by the Qin, see Derk Bodde, *China's First Unifier: A Study of the Ch'in Dynasty as Seen in the Life of Li Ssu* (Leiden: E. J. Brill, 1938): 22-4, 162-6.

36. Wang's own moral enlightenment occured during a time of deep isolation, when he unjustly was banished to Guizhou. So, in his own case, the moral conviction arose *out of* isolation. I owe this observation to Betsy Lancefield.

37. Cf. Chan, *Instructions*, section 181.

# 顔元

# 6. Yan Yuan

Like many other Neo-Confucian thinkers, Yan Yuan[1] (1635-1704 C.E.) studied a broad range of traditions. For example, as a young adult, he strictly observed Daoist practices.[2] But in time he declared his allegiance to Confucianism. The course of his intellectual development was leading him along a familiar trajectory and toward becoming a respected member of the Cheng-Zhu School, until, at the age of thirty-three, the death of his foster grandmother precipitated a radical turn in his life and thought.

In grieving for his foster grandmother, Yan committed himself to observing every detail of proper ritual mourning[3] as described by the renowned and revered *Jiali* 家禮 "Family Ritual," attributed to Zhu Xi.[4] But the extreme difficulty that he experienced in attempting to follow certain of the *Jiali*'s prescriptions, led him to compare its recommendations to classical discussions of ritual. Much to his surprise and dismay, he discovered a number of significant discrepancies that opened a growing vein of doubt concerning the reliability of Song and later Ming Confucian teachings. In time, this doubt blossomed into the complete rejection and pointed criticism of Song and Ming Confucians for being at odds with the classics, fatally tainted with Buddhist and Daoist elements and out of touch with the practical human concerns at the heart of the Confucian tradition.

Yan Yuan became convinced that both the Cheng-Zhu and Lu-Wang schools had lost sight of and severely distorted the original teachings of Kongzi, and he called for a return to and restoration of what he believed was Kongzi's true and original vision. In calling for a return to a past golden age, Yan sounded a classical Confucian theme. For Confucians have always looked back to an ideal past for guidance and inspiration. As we have seen in the earlier chapters of this volume, since the death of Kongzi, Confucian thinkers focused as much upon his teachings and examples—both real and imagined—as upon those of the sage kings of old. And since at least as early as the time of Xunzi, they have seen threats to their Way both within as well as outside their own tradition. In all these respects, Yan Yuan represented mainstream, traditional Confucian concerns.

Because his philosophical reflection was motivated by a break with orthodoxy, Yan tended to present his philosophical views in the course of advancing criticisms of prevailing Confucian belief and practice. Such an approach also makes sense given his fundamentally traditionalist perspective. He sought to revive and defend an ancient vision; he was not attempting to describe a novel opinion of his own design. Many of Yan's objections can be seen as part of an increasingly strong turn away from the speculative metaphysics that had characterized the Song (960-1279 C.E.) and Ming dynasties (1386-1644 C.E.)—the ages of Zhu Xi and Wang Yangming, respectively—and toward the more philologically and historically rigorous approach to the classics, that would become the hallmark of the Qing dynasty (1644-1911 C.E.).[5] However, Yan did not develop the more elaborate philological methods and theories that were the mark of these later Confucian thinkers; he remained steadfastly dedicated to ritual practice and a more physical approach to self cultivation.

Yan's primary motivation for criticizing his Confucian predecessors and contemporaries was always close to the surface of his philosophical writings. Put simply, he was frustrated and impatient with their failure to bring about the successful transformation of society. Like other Chinese intellectuals of his age, the collapse of the Ming and the founding of the Qing dynasty by the non-Chinese Manchus had a profound effect on Yan Yuan's thinking. Contrary to the explicit and often proclaimed goal of Confucian practice, Chinese society was anything but peaceful, orderly, and flourishing; it had decayed and been overcome by "barbarian" invaders. Yan Yuan believed that the teachings and practices of Song and Ming Confucians, and their followers in his own age, were directly responsible for this sad turn of events. They had allowed Chinese culture to become weak and incapable of fending off these foreign invaders. And so their way surely could not be the Way.

One possible response to this aspect of Yan Yuan's thought would be to point out that on such practical criteria, Kongzi himself would not have fared very well. For Kongzi too had failed to bring about the return to the golden age of the Zhou that was his guiding vision and goal. But Yan Yuan insisted that there were important differences between Kongzi's case and the case of these later, Neo-Confucians. Kongzi had been denied an opportunity to put his teachings into practice, while Song and Ming Confucians had had ample opportunity to influence the course of political and social events.[6] Instead of producing a new golden age, their policies had proved disastrous for China. Worse still, these Confucians were pompous and complacent about their failure and seemed oblivious to how empty their teachings had become. In Yan Yuan's words,

> When I tried to make sense of the teachings of Song Confucians, it was like blowing up a pig's bladder. All I could do was make something small and trifling into something large and empty.[7]

Yan argued that there was an irreconcilable and important difference between Song and Ming Confucians and Kongzi and that a confusion of their distinct and very different cases was at the heart of later Confucian misconceptions about the Way. To believe, as later Confucians had done, that one's historical situation and particular mission are just like those of Kongzi, is symptomatic of a particular kind of muddle. Later Confucians had fundamentally misunderstood what Kongzi had taught because they mistook what he was *forced* to do by the particular historical circumstances that he faced, as what he advocated as the ideal form of learning and practice.

> The reason why, since the time of the Han and Song Dynasties, the Way has not been clearly understood, is because people have misunderstood what the word *xue* 學 "learning" means. Since they have been mistaken about what learning is, how could they not be mistaken about what proper *xi* 習 "practice" consists in? And since they are mistaken about both learning and practice, how could they understand *dao* 道 "the Way?". . .
>
> People only see Kongzi's narrating the *History*, passing on the *Rites*, editing the *Odes*, correcting the *Music*, elaborating the *Changes*, and composing the *Spring and Autumn Annals*. They don't realize that Kongzi intended all of these works as guides designed to enable one to regulate and perfect one's practice in order to bring order to the world and benefit to the people. He hoped that people in later ages would follow these methods and put them into practice. Instead [later Confucians] mistakenly came to believe that to be a sage, one must compose and edit various writings and to be a worthy, one must pass down and annotate different texts. They thought that those who are widely read, clear in providing explanations and proficient in composition are all true disciples of Kongzi. As a result the last two thousand years have been empty and useless.[8]

Yan Yuan admits what was accepted as fact: that Kongzi himself engaged in scholarly, written work. He edited, amended, elaborated upon, and transmitted the classical texts of the tradition. But contrary to what later Confucians came to believe, this had nothing to do with his method of self cultivation. In fact, this more scholarly work is something he turned to—and could succeed at—only *after* he had mastered the ancient ways through diligent and protracted practice of ritual and passed through the experience of teaching these things to his disciples. Kongzi turned to his scholarly work of editing and transmitting the classics only at the end of his life, when it became clear to him that no ruler was going to employ him and allow him to put the Way into practice in his own age. Kongzi's scholastic achievements were something he did as a last resort, something he was forced to do by historical circumstances.⁹ Song and Ming Confucians and their contemporary followers foolishly and tragically took Kongzi's textual labors as the core of his teachings on self cultivation. And so they engaged in scholarly pursuits at the expense of more concrete learning, and never mastered the real and requisite skills of the sage. The result is all too evident—Confucians had become a pathetic flock of feckless scholastics.

> From the time of the Song and Yuan Dynasties (1280-1385 C.E.), Confucians have worked at becoming like women. It is terribly disgraceful! With nothing to do, they sit with their hands in their sleeves and discuss *xin* 心 "the mind" and *xing* 性 "human nature." When danger comes, all they can manage to do for their lord is to find some way to die.¹⁰

> Of those who these days sit straight-laced and dignified in their studies, none are not fragile and weak, the laughingstock of soldiers and farmers. Is this how men should be?¹¹

Not even friends escaped Yan's withering criticism.

> My friend Zhang Shiqing is broadly read in every kind of literature. He himself says that of the literary and historical works of the Qin (221-207 B.C.E.) and Han Dynasties (206 B.C.E.-8 C.E. and 25-220 C.E.) on down through the last two thousand years, none has escaped his notice. He works to explain the meaning of these texts to his young students until his strength is exhausted and he must rest in bed. After lying there panting for some time, he rises to resume his lecture until his strength is again exhausted.¹²

This confusion in both the content and style of true learning was the source of the tradition's decay. Yan Yuan offers an ingenious genealogical account of how this error arose and took hold that both diagnoses the problem and points the way back to proper understanding and practice. His narrative turns on a purported philological slippage that occurred—as most such things are wont to do—over the course of time. The crux of his argument is the claim that later Confucians misunderstood the sense of the character *wen* 文 in its classical context. This character has a long and rich history, extending al¹ the way back to designs found on Neolithic pottery.¹³ Its earliest sense was something like "pattern" or "form" and this early sense gave rise to the related meanings of "writing"¹⁴ and "culture."¹⁵ But Yan Yuan insists that, in the classical texts, the common and primary meaning of this character is "culture"—broadly construed. The later Confucian thinkers he criticizes went awry in regularly and mistakenly reading it as meaning "writing."

Those Han and Song Confucians only regard various collections of writing as *wen* 文 "culture." On such a view, then Yu and all the great sages and worthies who lived prior to the Xia Dynasty all were ignorant, base, and without any real learning. . . . But culture is not just the *Odes*, *History* and the Six Arts; an impressive personal presence, clear speech, the military, farming, hydraulics, the use of fire, finance, grain, labor, and risk—anything that can refine who I am and embellish the fundamental forces in the universe—all are part of culture![16]

Earlier, Wang Yangming had bemoaned the degree to which the Confucians of his age had focused on the letter rather than the spirit of the Way. He believed that this obsessive concern with words led people away from the "pure-knowing" of their own minds and gave rise to a variety of selfish desires. Wang argued that Kongzi himself was not concerned with the written word to the degree that the members of the Cheng-Zhu school were; because of the extreme, context-sensitive nature of ethical decisions, Kongzi did not want to rely on words at all.

Yan Yuan developed a version of this line of criticism, but in his own novel and distinctive way. He agreed with Wang about the overly scholastic approach of the Cheng-Zhu School, but rejected Wang Yangming's heroic metaphysical views about an originally pure and perfect moral mind, which constantly guides us through "pure knowing."[17] Yan Yuan even regarded Zhu Xi's more moderate conception of the mind as a combination of *li* and *qi* or, expressed differently, as having two modes—the "*dao* mind" and the "human mind"—as deeply misguided.[18] He regarded all such talk as overly abstract and ultimately just Buddhism in Confucian garb. Such grand metaphysical speculations, along with the excessive study of books, only served to generate unending and pointless scholastic debates. These led people away from concrete practice and toward a passive, inactive, and overly cerebral form of life.[19]

When the Confucian school talks about "broad learning"[20] they mean to learn ritual, music, archery, charioteering, writing and mathematics[21] and extend this to classics like the *Changes* and *History*. In regard to these things they always say "learn" them. When they talk about the Zhou Nan and Shao Nan,[22] they always say "do" [i.e., recite and practice] them. What the Confucian school means by learning and doing cannot be confused with what later generations call reading and discussing nor can ritual, music, archery, charioteering, writing, and mathematics be equated with commentaries and punctuation.[23]

Yan also rejected quiet sitting as another obvious case of Buddhist influence. Like metaphysical speculation, it too led to inactivity, and all it ever produced were useless illusions.

> That extreme calm can give rise to enlightenment is what the Buddhists call the "ultimate and extreme mystery." But in reality all such impressions are like the reflections of flowers in a mirror or the moon on water—they only exist upon the vacuous surface [of the mirror and water]. If you try to illuminate something with the image of the moon or pluck the flowers, it will not work.[24]

Yan Yuan responded to these bad tendencies within the Confucian tradition by trying to fuse together Neo-Confucian ideas about *li* and *qi* in a way that made it impossible to conceive of self cultivation as primarily a matter of "preserving" an original and perfectly pure endowment of *li* "principle" and "purifying" and guarding against the errant tendencies of our actual physical natures, i.e., our endowments of *qi*.[25] In order to undermine earlier descriptions of the relationship between *li* and *qi*, he offered an analogy between the "principle" of vision and the physical organ of sight.

> The eye presents a good analogy. The socket, eyeball, and pupil are *qizhi* 氣質 "physical stuff." The brightness within these that is able to see things is *xing* 性 "nature." But can one then go on to say that the *li* 理 "principle" of vision sees only what is correct while the socket, eyeball, and pupil see only what is perverse? I regard the principle of vision as indeed endowed by Heaven. But the socket, eyeball, and pupil are also all endowed by Heaven. And so there is no point to distinguishing what is *tianming zhi xing* 天命之性 "Heavenly endowed nature" from what is *qizhi zhi xing* 氣質之性 "physical nature." It is proper simply to say that Heaven endows people with the nature of the eye. . .[26]

Yan was seeking for a way to ensure that the focus of self cultivation would always consist in reshaping and training the physical human body and so he fought any tendency to conceive of our nature—and especially the good elements or aspects of it—as in any way separated from our physical embodiedness. He saw Song and Ming Confucians as the main proponents of precisely this kind of mistaken conception. Such views and practices departed from what Yan Yuan regarded as the proper early Confucian emphasis on the body and regular physical practice. The more ethereal, speculative theories of Song and Ming Confucians had eviscerated the tradition and enervated its later followers.

Yan Yuan advocated a method of learning that in important respects resembles Xunzi's *re-formation model*. Like Xunzi, he believed that self cultivation was very much an outside-in affair. One acquired virtue through repeated and concerted practice and inculcation, the accumulated effect of which shaped and transformed the self. Such a view entails a reverential attitude toward traditional norms, practices, and models, and so Yan was, like Xunzi, a cultural conservative. But there are significant differences between these two thinkers as well. While Xunzi endorsed the hands-on practice of the rites, he did not elevate the martial aspects of the tradition to the status they enjoy in Yan's writings. While Yan Yuan was clearly reacting to the more literary spirit of his and earlier times, as well as to the victory of the Manchus and other "barbarian" invaders, the result was a very physical—even macho—form of Confucianism.

> Are you not aware of the fact that within Kongzi's school, they were never without their bows and arrows, their swords and scabbards, even in times of peace, and that dancing the War Dance,[27] with battle axes and shields, was always a part of their course of learning?[28]

It is also important to note that Yan did not share Xunzi's view that human nature is bad; he explicitly endorsed and defended Mengzi's competing theory that human nature is good. Another difference between Xunzi and Yan Yuan concerns their respective views about the role that the intellect plays in the process of self cultivation. While Yan endorsed the study of classical texts, he does not manifest Xunzi's subtle appreciation of how, at more advanced levels of cultivation, a theoretical understanding of ritual and social norms plays an important role in shaping the self and justifying one's commitment to the Confucian Way.[29] Yan tends to show a much greater and comprehensive faith in the efficacy of ritual practice. Given these different features of his position, and particularly the preeminent status of ritual practice, I will refer to Yan Yuan's view as the *praxis model* of self cultivation.

Yan Yuan supported his general view of the tradition by showing how it relates to and explains a range of problems at the heart of Confucian philosophal debate in his time. For example, according to Yan, the true meaning of the term *gewu* 格物 supports the kind of hands-on practice of the traditional rites and related Confucian disciplines that he advocated. Contrary to what the Cheng-Zhu School maintained, to engage in *gewu* is not to discover some rarefied thing called principle, nor is it, as Wang Yangming claimed, to rectify one's thoughts. Rather, it is to *ge* "reach into" *wu* "things" by mastering the daily practice of the rites and norms of the Confucian way. That is to say, it was not a theoretical discipline leading to understanding but a practical process that resulted in know-how.

One can understand Yan's view as a claim about what it takes to arrive at the same goal Zhu Xi and Wang Yangming worked toward—Confucian sagehood. But for Yan the unity of knowledge and action was realized when one gained the kinds of abilities that come only from reflective practice of a craft. As with the earlier thinkers whose thought we have explored, the main difference of opinion among these later Confucians concerns how to practice and realize a generally agreed-upon goal. Yan Yuan believed that Zhu Xi did not emphasize hands-on practice and practical problem solving enough while Wang failed to appreciate how much one must acquire from traditional norms and methods of practice.

Yan Yuan also insisted that his praxis model illustrated that the true and original meaning of the word *jing* 敬 "reverence" is more common-sensical than what Neo-Confucians—and in particular Zhu Xi—had claimed. Recall that for Zhu Xi *jing* meant something like "reverential attention." He described it as the state of mind that one needed to be in in order to ensure that one's practice would be efficacious. Zhu Xi's conception of *jing* gave him a way of uniting the practices of *cunxin* "preserving the mind" and *dao wenxue* "pursuing inquiry and study."[30] According to Zhu Xi, these practices described efforts directed at two aspects or modes of the mind: the original mind and its subsequent activities. Yan rejected this elaborate and elegant scheme and insisted that *jing* simply meant to be focused on and serious about what one was doing. He accused Zhu Xi of importing Buddhist ideas into the original Confucian conception of seriousness and thereby divorcing it from its context of everyday practice.

The word *jing* "seriousness" is nice to look at, but its meaning has been obscured and corrupted by the influence of Chan Buddhism. The ancients taught [their students] to clean the floors and to clean them with a serious frame of mind. They taught them to respond to questions, to advance and retire, and to do these things with a serious frame of mind. They taught ceremonies, music, archery, charioteering, writing, and mathematics, instructing their students to determine the appropriate grade of ritual, set the proper musical pitch, shoot with resolute and settled intention, control the team with precision, compose each character with care, and solve every problem of multiplication and division precisely—to perform all of these tasks with a serious frame of mind. . . . And so it is said, "Be serious when carrying out your official assignments."[31] "Be serious in serving your ruler."[32] "Be careful and serious in your conduct."[33]

In all these tasks, and in everything one does, in body and in mind, one must be serious in every respect. But if one abandons the established methods of the ancients, and describes seriousness only in terms of quiet sitting, composing oneself, walking sedately, and speaking slowly, this is to use our Confucian word "seriousness" to do the work of Buddhism. Far indeed is this from the Way![34]

Such was Yan Yuan's diagnosis of the problems plaguing his age. But what treatment did he prescribe for these maladies? Essentially he advocated a return to simple, concrete practice. Yan did not conceive of moral self cultivation in terms of discovering and manifesting the *li* "principles" within the mind or engaging some innate capacity. He believed that the classics and traditional rituals contained the lessons for the acquisition of sagehood and the idea was to assiduously practice these lessons.[35] Sageliness was like a skill or a craft, one needed to study and practice in order to acquire it.

In one of many memorable passages, Yan Yuan compares mastering the Way to mastering the playing of the lute.[36] Clearly, he insists, one cannot master playing the lute by merely making a study of an instruction book about how to play the lute. In order to master the lute, one must actually pick it up and practice playing it, and one must do so until every nuance of the music it can produce flows forth effortlessly and without reflection from a heart that is well trained, harmonious, and in tune. Yan Yuan believed that the Song Confucians went so far as to confuse the classics (the instruction book) for the Way itself (the skillfulness or virtue of the sage). But the classics are not the *Dao*; they are books about the *Dao*.[37] In terms of his analogy with lute playing, the Song Confucians confuse the instruction book for the virtuoso skill of the master lute player. But the book itself does not produce the beautiful strains of the lute, only one who has mastered the instrument can do that. In the same way the classics are not the *Dao*; the actions of sages constitute the Way.

In another telling analogy, Yan Yuan illustrates this point by comparing self cultivation to the art of medicine—a profession he once pursued and considered as a career.[38] He draws out and focuses upon the distinction between those who know about the art of healing and those who know how to heal.

Medicine provides a good analogy. Huang Di's *Suwen*, along with the *Jingui* and the *Yuhan* are all works that make clear the principles of medicine.[39] But if one wants to heal the afflicted and save the world, then one must go out and feel pulses, prepare medicine, and apply acupuncture, cauterization, massage, and pressure. Now there are deluded individuals who only work at gaining an extensive command of medical books. After they are well versed in the details of such works, they consider themselves to be world authorities on medicine. They regard feeling pulses, preparing medicine, and applying acupuncture, cauterizaton, massage, and pressure as mere "techniques" not worthy of study. Their collections of books grow broader each day and their understanding of them more refined. Everyone praises them and the whole world seeks to imitate them. The Qi Bo's and Huang Di's fill the world, and yet sick people lie side by side and the dead follow one another in succession![40]

Yan wanted Confucians to be practicing physicians, healers of their age, not scholars who could discuss the history of the profession. He insisted that the Confucian Way, like traditions of music and medicine, are disciplines that one must master through prolonged and concerted effort. "Studying" these disciplines involves practice, and "knowing" them entails special kinds of "know-how." While Yan tends to emphasize the role of practice to the detriment of theory, there is a sensible intuition at the heart of his ideal that is reflected in our own way of talking about what is now the profession of medicine; we too say that physicians *practice* their vocation.

Like others among his contemporaries, Yan Yuan was reacting to the proliferation of highly abstract and increasingly arcane philosophical speculation that had become the norm in his age. He believed strongly in the idea that people acquire virtue as a result of the daily practices that they pursue over time—what Alexis de Tocqueville called the "habits of the heart."[41] It is easy to understand his impatience with those who ignored such practical endeavors and instead argued over subtle points of speculative philosophy during periods when China had lost or was losing ground to foreign invaders and the society was in turmoil. Like others before him, an underlying belief in the truth and the efficacy of Confucianism led him to identify improper methods of self cultivation as the ultimate source of these difficulties and to look back to the early tradition for guidance and inspiration. The result was an invigorating, even muscular form of Confucianism.

# Notes

1. Yan Yuan is also known as Yan Xizhai 習齋. For a dated but still helpful introduction to his life and thought, see Mansfield Freeman, "Yen Hsi-chai: A 17th Century Philosopher," *Journal of the North China Branch of the Royal Asiatic Society*, 57 (1926): 70-91. Fung Yu-lan describes several important aspects of Yan's philosophy in his *A History of Chinese Philosophy*, vol. 2, Derk Bodde, tr., reprint (Princeton, NJ: Princeton University Press, 1973): 631-50. See also the entry on Yan Yuan in Arthur

W. Hummel, ed., *Eminent Chinese of the Ch'ing Period,* vol. 2 (Washington, DC: United States Government Printing Office, 1944): 912-5. For an important essay criticizing modern attempts to appropriate Yan Yuan's thought as "materialistic," "revolutionary," "scientific," "pragmatic," etc., see Tu Wei-ming, "Yen Yuan: From Inner Experience to Lived Concreteness," in his collection, *Humanity and Self-Cultivation: Essays in Confucian Thought* (Berkeley, CA: University of California Press, 1979): 186-215.

2. For example, when he married, in 1649, he did not sleep with his wife because he was observing Daoist longevity practices that prohibit sexual activity. See Yan's *Nianpu, sui* 15.

3. Yan Yuan did so in the mistaken belief that he was a member of the family surnamed Zhu. His mourning was so extreme that it endangered his health and led a member of the Zhu clan to disclose his true parentage. Yan resolved to use his true surname but deferred doing so until after the death of his foster grandfather, five years later.

4. For a translation of this important work, see Patricia B. Ebrey, tr., *Chu Hsi's Family Rituals: A Twelfth-century Chinese Manual for the Performance of Cappings, Weddings, Funerals, and Ancestral Rites* (Princeton, NJ: Princeton University Press, 1991).

5. For an important early work describing this turn, see Liang Ch'i-ch'ao, *Intellectual Trends in the Ch'ing Period,* Immanuel Hsu, tr. (Cambridge, MA: Harvard University Press, 1959). For a more recent study, see Yü Ying-shih, "Some Preliminary Observations on the Rise of Ch'ing Confucian Intellectualism," *Tsing Hua Journal of Chinese Studies* 11 (1975): 101-46. The most thorough and revealing introduction to this aspect of Qing thought and culture can be found in Benjamin Elman, *From Philosophy to Philology: Intellectual and Social Aspects of Change in Late Imperial China* (Cambridge, MA: Harvard University Press, 1990).

6. Among later commentators on the *Analects,* it was fairly common to invoke the idea that Kongzi's "not gaining an official position" offered an explanation for why he "transmitted rather then created" (*Analects* 7.1; cf. *Zhongyong* chapter 30.1). One finds further precedents for this notion in passages like *Analects* 8.14, 14.27 and *Zhongyong* chapter 28.

7. *Nianpu, sui* 30.

8. *Sishu zhengwu* 四書正誤 "Correcting Mistakes Regarding the *Four Books,"juan* 3 in *Yan Yuanji* 顏元記 (Beijing: Zhonghua shuju, 1987): 174-5.

9. See Mansfield Freeman, tr., *Preservation of Learning* (Los Angeles, CA: Monumenta Serica of the University of California, 1972): 143-4. A similar explanation would later be advanced and used as a criticism of fellow Confucians by the Qing dynasty thinker Zhang Xuecheng. However Zhang extends this line of thought by adding interesting claims concerning the need

to grasp earlier and contemporary historical contexts in order to truly understand the *Dao*. For a discussion of Zhang's views, see David S. Nivison, *The Life and Thought of Chang Hsüeh-ch'eng 1738-1801* (Stanford, CA: Stanford University Press, 1966): 149-52.

10. *Cunxue bian* 存學編 "Preserving Learning," *juan* 1 in *Yan Yuanji*, p. 51.

11. *Cunxue bian, juan* 3 in *Yan Yuanji*, p. 73.

12. *Cunxue bian, juan* 3 in *Yan Yuanji*, p. 73. Xunzi also criticizes decadent Confucians for being physically weak and wimpy. For example, "Evasive and timorous, disliking work, lacking integrity, shameless, interested only in food and drink, they insist that 'a gentleman naturally would not engage in manual labor'—such are the base Ru of the school of Ziyou." Translation from John Knoblock, *Xunzi*, vol. 1, p. 229. Thanks to Eric Hutton for pointing out this passage to me.

13. For examples of such patterns on pottery, see K. C. Chang, *Art, Myth and Ritual: The Path to Political Authority in Ancient China* (Cambridge, MA: Harvard University Press, 1983): 83. For a discussion see pages 84-5.

14. Myth has it that Cang Jie invented writing by looking at the *wen* "patterns" of bird tracks and that this discovery marked the beginning of true culture. For a discussion of this account of the invention of writing, see Mark Edward Lewis, *Writing and Authority in Early China* (Albany, NY: SUNY Press, 1999): 272-4. Lewis also discusses the myth of Cang Jie and its relationship to earlier stories about Fu Xi's discovery of the trigrams of the *Yijing* on pages 199, 201, and 208. Lewis's work provides a magisterial study of the role written works played in legitimating authority in early China.

15. Chinese characters, especially when written with a brush, are aesthetic forms as well as a means for recording language. The degree to which Chinese culture evolved around this evocative written form further blends the senses in which *wen* can mean "pattern," "writing," and "culture."

16. *Sishu zhengwu, juan* 3 in *Yan Yuanji*, p. 190. Yu was the last of the early mythical sage-kings and founder of the Xia dynasty whose traditional dates are 2205-1766 B.C.E. The Six Arts composed Kongzi's basic curriculum. They were: ritual, music, archery, charioteering, writing, and mathematics. Yan's point is that Yu and other sage-kings, such as Yao, Shun, and early cultural heroes such as Fu Xi, Huang Di, and Shen Nong all lived long before the classics were composed. If "culture" is conceived of primarily in terms of such "writings," then most of the greatest figures in the tradition must have been bereft of culture.

17. For Wang's views about the mind, see pp. 60, 68.

18. For these aspects of Zhu Xi's thought, see pp. 47-9.

19. See Freeman, *Preservation of Learning*, p. 119 for an example of this

kind of criticism.

20. Here Yan is glossing a line from *Analects* 6.25, "[The master] broadens me with *wen 'culture.'*"

21. i.e., The Six Arts. See note 16.

22. The Zhou Nan and Shao Nan are the first two sections of the *Odes* and are often used to refer to the entire text.

23. *Cunxue bian, juan* 4 in *Yan Yuanji,* p. 97.

24. *Cunxue bian, juan* 2 in *Yan Yuanji,* p. 69. For another passage that compares such Chan-like practices to Song Confucians, see *Sishu zhengwu, juan* 3 in *Yan Yuanji,* p. 191.

25. Fung Yu-lan offers a good description of Yan's attempt to fuse the earlier distinction between *li* and *qi* and why ultimately it did not succeed. See *A History of Chinese Philosophy,* pp. 644-7.

26. *Cunxing bian* 存性編 "Preserving Human Nature," *juan* 1 in *Yan Yuanji,* p. 1.

27. For a description, see James Legge, tr., *The Chinese Classics, Vol. 3, The Shoo King,* reprint (Hong Kong: Hong Kong University Press, 1970): 66.

28. *Cunxue bian, juan* 2 in *Yan Yuanji,* p. 58.

29. Yan was criticized for taking his emphasis on practice too far and failing to see the importance of theory by later Confucians. See Benjamin Elman, *From Philosophy to Philology: Intellectual and Social Aspects of Change in Late Imperial China,* p. 51.

30. See pp. 49-52.

31. *Analects* 13.19.

32. *Analects* 15.37.

33. *Analects* 15.5.

34. *Cunxue bian, juan* 4 in *Yan Yuanji,* p. 91. The four practices Yan describes were followed by Neo-Confucians as ways of cultivating "reverence." Yan implies that there is an obvious parallel between these and Chan practices designed to cultivate "mindfulness."

35. At one point, Yan criticizes Song Confucians as those who "create rather than transmit, who really do not trust in and love the ancients." Thus they are the mirror image of what Kongzi describes in *Analects* 7.1. For a discussion of the passage in the *Analects,* see p. 1. For Yan Yuan's remark, see *Sishu zhengwu, juan* 3 in *Yan Yuanji,* p. 191.

36. See Freeman, *Preservation of Learning,* pp. 145-6.

37. Here again we find an issue and line of inquiry that is later pursued

by Zhang Xuecheng. For a discussion, see Nivison, *The Life and Thought of Chang Hsüeh-ch'eng 1738-1801*, pp. 150-1.

38. Yan began to study medicine in 1656 (see *Nianpu, sui* 22) and began to practice around two years later (see *Nianpu, sui* 24).

39. Huang Di, along with Qi Bo below, are ancient paragons of the medical profession and co-authors of the *Suwen*. The *Jingui* and *Yuhan* are other early works on the art of healing.

40. *Cunxue bian, juan* 1 in *Yan Yuanji*, p. 50. Cf. Freeman, *Preservation of Learning*, pp. 81-2.

41. Alexis de Tocqueville, *Democracy in America*, George Lawrence, tr., J. P. Mayer, ed. (New York: Doubleday Anchor Books, 1969), p. 287. For a contemporary study of American habits of the heart, see Robert Bellah et al., *Habits of the Heart: Individualism and Commitment in American Life*, reprint (New York: Harper and Row Publishers, 1986) and *The Good Society* (New York: Vintage Books, 1992).

戴震

# 7. Dai Zhen

Dai Zhen (1723-1777 C.E.) is the best known and most respected thinker of China's last imperial dynasty, the Qing (1644-1911 C.E.).[1] His intellectual contributions are remarkable in their breadth alone; he produced significant works on mathematics, astronomy, geography, philology, phonetics, and philosophy. He is best known for his philological studies and for his contributions to the Imperial Library Compilation known as the *Sikuquanshu* 四庫全書 "Complete Collection of the Four Treasuries."[2] I will focus on an aspect of his work for which he was neither well known nor particularly respected, at least in his own lifetime: his ethical philosophy.[3] In particular, in keeping with our stated theme, I will explore his view of moral self cultivation.

Dai's ethical philosophy is extremely original and distinctive among Confucian thinkers. This is probably why his contemporaries were a bit perplexed by this aspect of his thought and why he remains little understood or appreciated even in our own time. Unlike other Neo-Confucians, Dai did not espouse the assiduous practice of rites; he did not practice or advocate a life of constant inner scrutiny, nor did he engage in quiet sitting. His method of self cultivation was much more cerebral or academic in character. He saw moral improvement exclusively as an intellectual, scholarly endeavor. Dai was never a moral teacher, in the style of Zhu Xi; much less was he a kind of spiritual *guru* in the manner of Wang Yangming. He was a rather withdrawn and bookish person, but one who had a genuine intellectual passion for moral knowledge. And if he was right in believing that a proper understanding of the classics was the key to moral improvement, there would be little need or room for spiritual guides or gurus.[4]

Some interpreters of Dai's thought see a deep tension, if not an outright conflict, between his dual interests in ethical philosophy and philological studies.[5] I will argue that such an understanding of Dai's thought misses the essence of his philosophy. For Dai there was no genuine philosophy outside of philology, and true philology was *always* philosophical in nature. Philology was the very method of philosophy. The introduction to one of Dai's two main philosophical essays, the *Yuan Shan* 原善 "On the Good," shows that such a view was the motivation and guiding assumption of this important work.[6]

I first composed the *Yuan Shan* in three chapters [but] I feared that students would be misled by their individual interests, and so I drew supporting passages from the classics and used these to explain and verify my work. I separated the three chapters and made each of them an opening [section] and then supplemented each of these [with supporting passages from the classics] to form three books, grouping together material that agreed in kind and meaning so each point and every detail was clearly displayed.

The Ways of Heaven and human beings are revealed completely in the great lessons of the classics. But since the present age is so far removed from the wisdom of the sages of old, among those who study the classics, none is able to gain a comprehensive and thorough understanding of them. Habituated by what they see and hear, they accumulate falsehoods and turn them into "truths". . . .

Dai explains how he had originally written a rather speculative philosophical essay in three parts, concerning the central terms of art in Confucian thought. But he realized that in order to carry forth his argument, he needed to present evidence for the positions he described by quoting from the classics. Consequently, he divided up the original essay into three parts and used each of these to introduce extended examples drawn from various classical texts. It is possible to interpret Dai as saying that he used the classics to verify truths that he had arrived at through a process of philosophical reflection, but a careful reading of this preface and his other work shows that Dai believed that the process that led him to a true understanding of the Way worked in very much the opposite direction, it was *derived from* a proper understanding of the truths inscribed in the classics. For him, the projects of philosophy and philology were coextensive; one found the truth by getting the classics *right* and one got the classics right by doing careful textual work.

It is precisely because sheer speculation cannot lead one to the philosophical ideas of the sages of antiquity that one has to seek them from the ancient classics. Since messages contained in the surviving records have gradually fallen into oblivion due to the expanse of time between the past and the present, one therefore has to seek them through philological studies [of the classics]. Thus only if philology is clear, can the ancient classics be understood; and only if the classics are understood, c a n the sages' philosophical ideas then be grasped.[7]

This paragraph, as well as many other things that Dai said, can be understood as his particular interpretation of Kongzi's teaching that,

"Study without reflection is a waste. Reflection without study is a danger."[8] According to Dai, learning requires that one reflect on a specific corpus of texts in a specific way. One needs to reflect upon the classics in the sense of submitting them to careful, critical, and comprehensive philological analysis. Only in this way could one be sure of arriving at a proper understanding. "Reflection" in the sense of "sheer speculation" could only lead one astray. Once one appreciates this aspect of Dai Zhen's vision, one can see why he wrote the kinds of philosophical books he did and why he focused on the kinds of problems he chose to explore. Both the *Yuan Shan* and his magnum opus, the *Mengzi ziyi shuzheng* 孟子字義疏證 "The Meaning of Terms in the *Mengzi* Explained and Verified,"[9] are philological explorations of classical Confucian philosophy. These works were organized around two guiding aims: a refutation of contemporary *misunderstandings* of the classics and an *exposition* of the true meaning of these cherished texts. Dai was greatly concerned with disabusing the people of his age of their mistaken interpretations of the classics. He fervently believed that the views current in his age were deeply stained by Daoist and Buddhist influences, and he sought to expurgate these and return to the original meaning of the classics. These points are elegantly and powerfully made in the preface to the *Mengzi ziyi shuzheng*.

Mengzi disputed [the doctrines of] Yang and Mo. [But] later people are accustomed to hearing the doctrines of Yang, Mo, Laozi, Zhuangzi, and the Buddha. Moreover, they have used these doctrines to disrupt and confuse the doctrines of Mengzi. This is why those who come after Mengzi again cannot refrain [ f r o m engaging in debate].[10] Were I unable to understand this, then that would be the end of it. But to understand and not speak out—that would be disloyalty! I would be turning my back on the learning of the sages and worthies of old and distancing myself from the benevolence of the good people of my own age and those of later generations. Apprehensive about this, I composed the *Mengzi ziyi shuzheng*. Han Yü [11] said, "To follow the teachings of Yang, Mo, Lao, Zhuang, and the Buddha with the hope of reaching the Way of the sage, is like navigating a closed off harbor or cut off lake w i t h the hope of reaching the sea. And so, those who seek to gaze upon the Way of the sage must begin with Mengzi."

Dai was a strong ethical realist, and he believed that one approached moral truth by getting clear about the facts of the matter. The knowledge one gains through study leads to moral understanding. For him, self cultivation consisted in a systematic, critical, comprehensive, careful, and thorough study of the classics; in his own terms, study nourishes one's mind just as food nourishes one's body.[12] Dai expressed no interest in developing some nascent moral capacity, nor did he emphasize the need for shaping the self through ritual practice. He did not advocate cultivating and maintaining a state of constant inner vigilance, nor did he engage in practices such as quiet sitting. He is unique among the thinkers we have discussed thus far in that he believed that proper *intellectual* understanding was the only way to fully grasp the *Dao*.

In part, Dai's position was a reaction to the overly subjective approach of Neo-Confucianism, but it is also very much a manifestation of his own personality. As was mentioned, Dai was a rather bookish person who was constantly striving to perfect his own understanding of the many disciplines he practiced. One can see this tendency to constantly refine and enlarge his understanding in his philosophical work as well; he produced no less than four separate versions of his magnum opus, the *Mengzi ziyi shuzheng,* and would probably have produced more had he not died about a year after the last version was completed.

It is tempting to speculate about the effect that Dai's various intellectual pursuits had on his view of self cultivation. He was engaged in numerous disciplines that required sophisticated mathematical expertise and careful empirical method. It seems reasonable to see these as informing his methodology in both philology and philosophy. One perceives an almost scientific tendency in both his ethical philosophy and textual studies. In one's individual moral decisions, he argued that one must avoid taking one's *yijian* 意見 "opinion" as the truth. Instead, one must research and reason one's way to *buyi zhi ze* 不易之則 "unchanging standards." One employs the same method in textual studies: moving from one's initial impression of a text to a proper interpretation by continually revising one's idea about what it means in light of careful and comprehensive philological and historical study. Dai's approach to moral self cultivation can be understood as an ethical expression of the hermeneutical circle.

In regard to moral issues, one moves from opinion to truth by discovering those things that everyone would agree to do in a given situation, and one accomplishes this by employing the Confucian golden rule.[13]

> [Someone] asked, "What did the ancients mean by *Heavenly principle?*"
>
> [Dai] responded, "*Principle* is feelings that do not err. One can never be without the proper feelings and still grasp principle. Whenever one does something to another, one should turn within oneself and calmly consider, If another had done this to me would I be willing to accept it? Whenever one requests something of another, one should turn within oneself and calmly consider, If

another requested this of me would I be willing to do it? If one measures [one's treatment of] others with oneself, then principle will be clear."[14]

It is very important to grasp this aspect of Dai's thought, for it shows that while emphasizing the role of reason in moral self cultivation, he was by no means antagonistic toward desires or emotions. Quite the contrary, he saw, correctly, that certain of our shared desires serve as the very basis of Mengzi's moral philosophy, and that, on this view, there is no fundamental tension between our desires and morality. Our *true* desires, those which we possess when fully aware of what we are as creatures and how the world works, lead us to be moral. One of Dai's central complaints about Neo-Confucian thinkers was their failure to appreciate the role of desires.

> When the ancients talked about principle, they sought for it in human feelings and desires; they took following principle to be a matter of causing feelings and desires to be without flaw. When people today talk about principle, they seek for it apart from human feelings and desires; they take following principle to be a matter of causing oneself to endure yet be indifferent to feelings and desires. This distinction between principle and desire is just the thing that will turn the people of the world into deceivers and hypocrites.[15]

Dai's intellectual method of self cultivation is original and unique. He describes its trajectory by saying that we all start out with natural desires (what is *ziran* 自然 "natural"), and that the moral task is to transform these into moral desires (what is *biran* 必然 "necessary" or "imperative"). This is the process of moving from *yijian* "mere opinion" to *buyi zhi ze* "an unchanging standard." Mere opinions will be culled by passing one's "natural desires" through the winnowing standard of the Confucian golden rule. In this way, only *biran* "necessary" desires will be allowed to manifest themselves in actions. If my natural desires fully accord with what the golden rule commands, then they are not just opinions, they are necessities, things that I *must* do.

Dai's model of moral self cultivation strongly emphasizes the role of the intellect to *realize* the Way—both in the sense of recognizing what is right and directing the self to follow what is right. These two aspects of moral self cultivation appear to occur simultaneously in his view of things. And so it seems appropriate to refer to Dai's method as a *realization model* of moral self cultivation.

Though he criticizes them relentlessly, Dai is actually closer to Zhu Xi and Wang Yangming than he is to the early Confucians he claimed to defend and sought to emulate. First, like Zhu and Wang, Dai believes that we *already* possess appropriate moral feelings. The problem is that we also have many inappropriate feelings that obscure and interfere with those that are correct. In contrast, Mengzi believed that appropriate feelings need to be cultivated; our nascent sprouts must be strengthened, expanded, and extended in order to fulfill the demands of morality. Xunzi believed that appropriate feelings need to be acquired; we have some desires and feelings that can be conscripted into the moral cause but even these are like raw clay, in need of shape and texture. Second, for Dai our central problem is that we have too many feelings and need to weed out the inappropriate ones—those that are "mere opinion." For him, the process of self cultivation is a filtering-out of erroneous influences, namely, any thought, inclination, or desire that is *si* 私 "selfish." This is much closer to Zhu's or Wang's view than it is to any early Confucian. In general, Neo-Confucians saw moral self cultivation more as a paring-away of the bad rather than a building up of the good—however the later is conceived. What is distinctive about Dai is the degree to which he relies upon the intellect and specifically upon scholarly endeavor to achieve this end.

Given this picture of Dai's ethical philosophy, it would seem that he is not altogether clear about an issue that is central to Mengzi's theory of moral self cultivation. Recall that for Mengzi, morality is satisfying in the same way that good food and pleasant sights and sounds are satisfying. For him, a special kind of joy marks the moral act as moral. This joy also makes moral self cultivation possible, by providing positive reinforcement for the good actions one performs. Dai clearly endorses the idea that *any* moral action one does produces a feeling of joy, if only one reflects upon it.

> When Mengzi said, "Principle and righteousness please my mind just as the flesh of grass and grain fed animals pleases my palate," this was not a metaphor. Whenever one does something that accords with principle and righteousness, one's heart and spirit will always be joyful and contented.[16]

However, as we have seen, Dai believes that in order to *recognize* something as a case of principle or righteousness, one must already have passed it through the golden rule's universalizability test. It would seem that one can experience the joy of moral action only after one has discovered what is *necessary* and understands the *unchanging standard* behind one's action.[17]

And so Dai seems to require a second-order knowledge of the necessary moral standard in order to experience the joy of moral action. While Mengzi does believe that in order to appreciate the joy of moral action we must be aware of the fact that we are motivated by our moral sense, he does not seem to require the kind of abstract understanding Dai insists upon, as a prerequisite to experiencing the joy of moral action.[18] Perhaps the way to relieve this apparent tension within Dai's thought is to understand him as saying that we will enjoy every truly moral action that we perform, but we will only experience the *full joy* of such actions when we understand their underlying principles completely. Such a position, though not explicitly held by Mengzi, would seem to be consistent with his general picture of moral self cultivation.

Much of Dai's philosophical project involved a refutation of the views of thinkers like Zhu Xi and Wang Yangming. He believed that such thinkers had unknowingly incorporated Daoist and Buddhist ideas into the Confucian school and perverted its message. Dai relied upon rather straight-forward philological arguments in order to make his case against the Neo-Confucians. For example, he repudiated the notion that the mind contained *li* "principle" or that it is principle[19] by deploying careful philological arguments supported by extensive classical references.[20] He argued decisively and convincingly, that in the classical texts of Confucianism, the term *li* never had the kinds of senses that Neo-Confucians later ascribed to it According to Dai, Zhu and Wang had lost sight of the fact that *li* simply meant "good order." It is the orderly pattern of the universe which we can come to understand through careful examination and study. It is not *within us* already; it is something we come to realize through acquiring certain kinds of knowledge and augmenting this with a systematic application of the Confucian golden rule.

> In the Six Classics, the *Analects* and *Mengzi* and even in the various biographies and other records [from ancient times], one does not often see the character *li* "principle." But n o w a d a y s even the most ignorant people, no matter how perverse or dissolute, will quickly invoke the notion of *principle* whenever they decide an affair or upbraid another. Ever since the Song dynasty, it has become the common practice and established custom to regard *principle* as if it were a thing received from Heaven and lodged in the heart and mind, and to take the opinions of the heart and mind as according with principle.[21]

Dai Zhen had begun with a faith in the classics and the sages, and his careful, objective study of the language and history of these convinced him that the true meaning of the classics had been lost. He believed that he had arrived at their truth by relying on careful research and reasoning, and this in turn convinced him that the truth of the classics itself is rational and demonstrable. The truth of the classics must itself be an *unchanging standard*, something that is *necessary*. But if the classics themselves are simply a manifestation of this unchanging standard and one can arrive at this standard through the careful application of the Confucian golden rule, it would seem as if one should be able to realize the standard simply by appeal to the rule. Why would one need to proceed by way of the classics?

It seems as if Dai has climbed the ladder of the classics and could, at this point, very well have kicked it away. He did not, and it is clear why he did not; he never considered doing philosophy in any way other than *through* the classics. In this he remained true to some of the oldest promptings within the Confucian tradition. He saw his quest to discern the teachings of the sages as a task of *finding* not *making*, more a matter of *xue* "study" than *si* "reflecting." [22] For him, providing an account of *why* one does what one does is a task one can only approach *after* one has mastered the classics. It is only through such a course of study that one can *become* the kind of person who will make the right choices; this in turn provides one with the understanding necessary for discerning the pattern behind one's actions. In this respect, moral understanding is regarded as like the knowledge of a craft. For Dai, as for many Confucians, rules, such as the golden rule, were never regarded as free standing justifications for action. [23]

Because Dai relied on intellect over moral intuition, many scholars have likened him to Xunzi, and the comparison is neither unwarranted nor unhelpful. Yet we must recognize that, in respect to the classics and the sages, their philosophies are very different. Xunzi had faith that a calm and careful analysis of traditional rituals and norms would eventually convince anyone that they are the unique solution to life. But he insisted that one could only come to such an understanding by diligently *practicing* these traditional forms for many years under the strict discipline and guidance of a proper teacher. Those who are just beginning to learn the Way are largely unaware of the reasons that justify the things they practice. They are simply to obey their teachers and apply themselves diligently until they have enough experience and information to begin to see how the whole thing fits together. For Xunzi, one's *practice* of the *Dao* runs far ahead of one's *understanding* of it. For this reason, there was never any danger of dispensing with the lessons of the classics and the examples of the sages. Xunzi saw individual moral intuition as a threat to tradition. In particular, he worried that Mengzi was advocating a form of intuitionism that left no clear role for either the classics or the sages. [24]

In principle, it would seem that Dai Zhen is open to a similar charge, since he appears to have believed that one could *reason* one's way to moral truth through the careful application of the Confucian golden rule. Had he taken just one more step and regarded the rule as a decision procedure for generating only and all proper actions, he would have been open to such criticism; he might well have ended up following one influential steam of contemporary western ethical philosophy, a stream which has little interest in appeals to traditional wisdom. But Dai did not see things this way. He was very much a traditionalist and dedicated his life to discovering and making clear the genuine truths of the Confucian tradition and distinguishing these from the dross of Daoism and Buddhism. He never separated his ethical philosophical principle (universalizability) from his philology (the study of the classics). Had he done so, he might have seen some of the notorious problems that arise when one takes this final step, but had he taken it, he would no longer have been a traditional Confucian self cultivationist.

## *Notes*

1. For a brief biography of Dai Zhen, see "Tai Chen," in *Eminent Chinese of the Ch'ing Period (1644-1911)*, vol. 2, Arthur Hummel, ed. (Washington: Government Printing Office, 1943-44): 695-700. Brief descriptions of his philosophy with selected translations can be found in Chan, *Source Book*, pp. 709-22 and Fung, *History*, pp. 651-672. A general introduction, now quite dated, can be found in Mansfield Freeman, "The Philosophy of Tai Tung-yuan," *Journal of the North China Branch of the Royal Asiatic Society*, vol. 64 (1933): 50-71. See also the translations noted below.

2. For a good discussion of Dai's different kinds of work and his place in Chinese intellectual history, see Benjamin Elman, *From Philosophy to Philology* (Cambridge, MA: Harvard University Press, 1984).

3. Dai Zhen is still not well understood or appreciated as a philosopher. Wing-tsit Chan purportedly explains why Dai did not exert a great deal of influence in his own age by saying his doctrines "are not really profound." See Chan, *Source Book*, p. 711.

4. There was a fascinating and on going debate within the Confucian tradition regarding what the proper role and function of a teacher was. Many Confucians wrote essays with titles like *Shi shuo* 師說 "Discourse on Teachers" often criticizing earlier views and arguing for their own specific perspective. For an example of such an essay, see the translation of Han Yü's *Shi shuo* in Wm. Theodore de Bary, Wing-tsit Chan, and Burton Watson, *Sources of Chinese Tradition* (New York: Columbia University Press, 1960): 374-5.

5. For example, Yü Ying-shih argues that throughout his life, Dai was torn between the competing claims of philosophy and philology until in the end philosophy won out. See his "Tai Chen's Choice between Philosophy and Philology," *Asia Major*, n.s. 2.1 (1989): 79-108.

6. There is a translation of this work by Cheng Chung-ying, but unfortunately it is unreliable and obscures the structure and plan of the original text. See Cheng Chung-ying, tr., *Tai Chen's Inquiry into Goodness* (Honolulu, HI: East West Center Press, 1969).

7. Translation by Yü Ying-shih. See his "Tai Chen's Choice," pp. 83-4.

8. *Analects* 2.15. See Chapter 1, p. 2 and Chapter 3, p. 37.

9. There are several translations of this work now available. The most recent version is Ann-ping Chin and Mansfield Freeman, tr., *Tai Chen on Mencius: Explorations in Words and Meanings* (New Haven, CT: Yale University Press, 1990). This is generally an unreliable work. A much better translation is Torbjörn Lodén, tr., "Dai Zhen's Evidential Commentary on the Meaning of the Words of Mencius," *Bulletin of the Museum of Far Eastern Antiquities*, no. 60 (Stockholm: 1988): 165-313. The best translation of the text is by John W. Ewell, Jr., "Reinventing the Way: Dai Zhen's *Evidential Commentary on the Meanings of Terms in Mencius* (1777)" (Berkeley, CA: Unpublished PhD Dissertation in history, 1990).

10. Dai Zhen is drawing a comparison between himself and Mengzi as defenders of the faith who "could not but engage in disputation," the point being that neither he nor Mengzi was fond of disputation. See *Mengzi* 3B9. Cf. the discussion of Zhu Xi's relationship to Mengzi above, p. 43.

11. Han Yü (768-824 C.E.) is often considered to be one of the central figures in the revival of Confucianism. The quote is from a preface entitled *Song Wang xiucai* ("Parting Praise for Licentiate Wang") in *Han Changli quanji,* 20.7a-b (*SBBY*).

12. See section 9 of the *Mengzi ziyi shuzheng.*

13. Dai focused upon the notion of *shu* 恕 "sympathetic understanding," the ability to gauge what others desire by reflecting upon one's own desires. Cf. *Mengzi* 7A4.

14. See section 2 of the *Mengzi ziyi shuzheng.*

15. From section 43 of the *Mengzi ziyi shuzheng.*

16. *Mengzi ziyi shuzheng*, section 8. The quoted lines are from *Mengzi* 6A7.

17. This appears to be true at least for those who are starting out on the process of moral self cultivation. An individual who has developed a thorough and complete understanding of moral principles through a life of study and reflection, having formed her mind so that it is in complete accord with principle, might no longer need to engage in this intellectual exercise.

18. Mengzi's long exchange with King Xuan of Qi in *Mengzi* 1A7 shows that the king did not fully appreciate or enjoy his sparing of the ox until Mengzi led him to see that it was motivated by his moral sprouts.

19. The views of Zhu Xi and Wang Yangming, respectively.

20. For example, see sections 1 through 10 of the *Mengzi ziyi shuzheng*.

21. Section 5 of the *Mengzi ziyi shuzheng*.

22. Here again we can see Dai's views as elaborate reflections of one of Kongzi's basic teachings. In *Analects* 7.1, Kongzi insists that he is one who *shu er bu zuo* 述而不作 "transmits rather than creates." Cf. Chapter 1, p. 1.

23. I have argued that the golden rule can never provide such a freestanding justification for action. By itself, it proves inert; it must be embedded in a surrounding ethic in order to function effectively. See my "Reweaving the 'one thread' of the *Analects*."

24. As we have seen, this cannot be considered a fair criticism of Mengzi's position. However, it is not altogether inappropriate in the case of Wang Yangming; many of his later followers clearly took the idea of intuitionism to a radical extreme.

# Conclusion

This study of Confucian theories of moral self cultivation has ranged across a vast expanse of time and over an immensely rich cultural heritage. The dangers of such an ambitious undertaking are well rehearsed, but the potential rewards of such work need to be given their proper due. No one will deny that covering so many complex and varied thinkers in such a short work inevitably leaves out much of the depth, character, and texture of their philosophy. However, by focusing upon one specific aspect of their thought—their views on moral self cultivation—I have attempted to present some of the distinctive and vibrant features of their philosophy.[1] In addition, by presenting these thinkers as part of an extended dialogue over the nature and method of moral self cultivation, I have pointed out a way in which, as a tradition, these very different thinkers can be *joined with a single thread*.[2]

I began this work by arguing that some very old ideas about the nature of *de* "virtue"—in particular the human capacity to cultivate it and the role it plays in the establishment and functioning of a harmonious and flourishing society—tended to lead Chinese philosophers to be deeply concerned with the issue of moral self cultivation. I then proceeded to describe Confucius' *acquisition model* of moral self cultivation and noted that this model is consistent with either of two conflicting views: one claiming that moral virtue results from the proper cultivation of human nature, the other maintaining that it results from taking on a fundamentally artificial, second nature. The next thinker covered, Mengzi, advocated the former position, arguing that human nature was oriented and tended toward the good. Consequently, he proposed what I called a *developmental model* of moral self cultivation.

Mengzi's rival Xunzi championed the opposing view, arguing that human nature is basically bad. However, though having a rather negative view of what human beings naturally are and spontaneously tend toward, like Mengzi, Xunzi was quite optimistic about the possibility of what they might achieve. According to Xunzi, with enough training and reflection of the proper kind, one could transform one's raw nature and take on a second, moral nature. This, he believed, required one to redirect and reshape one's basic nature in profound and dramatic ways. Consequently, Xunzi proposed a *re-formation model* of moral self cultivation.

The next thinker I discussed, Zhu Xi, lived more than a thousand years after Xunzi's death and inhabited a very different intellectual landscape. He had different problems to solve and different tools with which to work. His intellectual world had absorbed and been transformed by a number of Daoist and Buddhist beliefs about the nature of the self and the world. From within this new perspective, the early Mengzian claim about the goodness of human nature was understood to mean that people had within them a fully formed and perfect moral mind. However, because of both the contingent fact of our physical embodiment and the errant behavior this tends to generate, most people had lost sight of this unerring source of moral knowledge. In order to find it again, they needed to engage in self cultivation.

For Zhu and other Neo-Confucian thinkers, to cultivate oneself was to bring forth the *li* "pattern" or "principle" inherent within one's moral mind.[3] This task was conceived largely in terms of casting out and polishing away those influences that obscured this inherent "pattern." For Zhu Xi, this required an elaborate and carefully conceived program of study, reflection, and meditation. He represents what I refer to as a *recovery model* of moral self cultivation.

Zhu's later critic, Wang Yangming, objected to this method on the grounds that it relied too much on "outside" support, e.g., the lessons of the classics, historical texts, and commentaries. Such an approach, Wang argued, directed one's attention away from the very thing one needed to succeed—one's innate moral mind. As an alternative, Wang proposed a radically context-sensitive method of moral self cultivation in which one was to concentrate on the events of one's own life and the movements of one's own mind. The goal was to learn to recognize and rely upon *liangzhi* "pure knowing," an innate and ever-ready faculty of moral perception and guidance. I refer to Wang's approach as a *discovery model* of moral self cultivation.

We then explored the thought of Yan Yuan, a thinker who lived from the late Ming through the early Qing dynasties. Yan Yuan reacted strongly against what he saw as the excessively speculative and largely ineffective teachings of Song and Ming Confucians. He believed that their overly cerebral and literary methods of self cultivation had led to the collapse of Chinese culture and the enervation of Confucians. Yan proposed a return to a more robust and practically oriented form of self cultivation. Instead of textual study, internal reflection, or quiet sitting, he wanted people to practice the rituals and master the practical arts of traditional Confucianism. Hence I describe him as advocating a *praxis model* of self cultivation.

The final thinker whose thought we explored, Dai Zhen, lived during China's last imperial dynasty. Like Yan Yuan, he criticized both Zhu Xi and Wang Yangming for straying from the original and true meaning of the classics by falling under the spell of Daoist and Buddhist influences. But, in stark contrast to Yan, Dai employed and advocated a very scholarly approach to self cultivation. Using sophisticated textual and philosophical analysis, Dai showed, quite convincingly, that Zhu, Wang, and other Neo-Confucians had read a great deal of Daoist and Buddhist metaphysics back into the early Confucian classics. He showed that much of the content and style of Neo-Confucianism was wholly foreign to the early thinkers its proponents claimed allegiance to and sought to defend.

Dai himself did not fully escape the influence of his age, for he shared a version of the later Confucian view that we possess a complete moral sense and only need to weed out those selfish influences which interfere with its smooth operation. However, in addition to revealing the extent to which the later Confucian tradition had drifted from its original moorings, Dai proposed a unique and remarkable view of how one might understand and bring into being the traditional Confucian goal of moral transformation. He argued that one needs to pass one's spontaneous reactions to things and events through the sieve of universalizability in order to filter out "mere opinions" and arrive at the "unchanging standard" of moral truth. Consequently, he proposed what I refer to as a *realization model* of moral self cultivation.

Following only *one thread* of the Confucian tradition has the inevitable consequence of ignoring many other important aspects of its grand design. However, any study of an ethical tradition should be judged in terms of what it adds to our understanding of the ethical problems the tradition explores and the particular approaches and sensibilities the members of the tradition bring to bear on these problems. If this work contributes to a greater appreciation of the distinctiveness of the Chinese Confucian concern with moral self cultivation and gives readers some sense of the variety, power, subtlety, and beauty of this aspect of Chinese philosophy, it will have fulfilled its purpose.

Beyond the immediate goal of helping us to better understand the Confucian tradition, I hope that this study contributes something to the larger project of stimulating contemporary ethical philosophers to think seriously about the issue of moral self cultivation. We must turn more of our attention and energy from theoretical to practical concerns and specifically to the question of how we and others can become better. To achieve such a goal we will have to pay greater attention to and cooperate more broadly with colleagues working in anthropology, history, education, psychology, sociology, and other related disciplines. Such interdisciplinary work is challenging and in some respects daunting, but in the case of these particular problems, it is necessary.

By providing a description and analysis of a particularly rich and vibrant ethical tradition, I hope that this study may also contribute to contemporary discussions about the nature and status of ethical traditions in general. These discussions bear directly upon issues such as whether anything like ethical truth exists, and they contain important implications for more distant debates such as the character and process of constitutional interpretation. Such discussions also lie at the very heart of other current controversies, for example, the question of what, if anything, should constitute the "canon" of a modern university.

The present study shows that the issues raised by such debates are neither new nor unique to the west. Facing such tensions and participating in such debates is part of what it means to be in a living ethical tradition. This work suggests that our attempts to reconcile these tensions will inevitably seem quaint, in at least some respects, if future generations should take the time to review them. Reflecting on this fact may engender a bit more humility, perhaps even some sense of irony, in those of us engaged in such current controversies. My hope is that it will lead us to produce less heat and more light.

Most important of all, this study suggests that in order to successfully address the ethical questions of one's own time and place, one needs not only an ideal toward which one should strive (some theoretical standard or goal), but also some conception of how one is to get there from here. Among other things, this requires one to have an understanding of the kind of creatures we are, what resources we begin with—our limitations as well as our capabilities—and how we might best put these to use. In other words, it requires one to take up the problems and join in the spirit of the Confucian tradition of moral self cultivation.

# Notes

1. As noted in the *Preface*, this work evolved out of a series of lectures that were written to appeal to experts and novices alike. The book has expanded the range of the lectures, filled in some of the historical gaps, and provided additional evidence from both original sources and specialized studies in the secondary literature. Still, it is by no means comprehensive or complete.

2. Cf. *Analects* 4.15 and 15.3. Needless to say, this is by no means the *only* thing these thinkers have in common.

3. As we have seen, Wang Yangming claimed the mind itself was principle.

# Works Cited

Allan, Sarah. *The Way of Water and Sprouts of Virtue.* Albany, NY: SUNY Press, 1997.

Ames, Roger T., and David L. Hall. *Thinking Through Confucius.* Albany, NY: SUNY Press, 1987.

Aristotle. *Nicomachean Ethics.* Terence Irwin, tr. Indianapolis, IN: Hackett Publishing Co. 1985.

Augustine. *The Confessions of Saint Augustine.* In *Basic Writings of Saint Augustine.* Vol. 1. Whitney J. Oakes , tr. New York: Random House, 1948.

Bellah, Robert, et al. *The Good Society.* New York: Vintage Books, 1992.

_____. *Habits of the Heart: Individualism and Commitment in American Life.* Reprint. New York: Harper and Row Publishers, 1986.

Berkson, Mark. "Review of *Two Chinese Philosophers.*" *Philosophy East and West* 45.2 (February, 1995): 292-97.

Bodde, Derk. *China's First Unifier: A Study of the Ch'in Dynasty as Seen in the Life of Li Ssu.* Leiden: E. J. Brill, 1938.

Bol, Peter K. *"This Culture of Ours:" Intellectual Transitions In T'ang and Sung China.* Stanford, CA: Stanford University Press, 1992.

Brooks, Bruce E., and Taeko A. Brooks. *The Original Analects: Sayings of Confucius and His Successors.* New York: Columbia University Press, 1998.

Bruce, J. Percy. *Chu Hsi and His Masters.* London: Probsthain, 1923.

Chan, Wing-tsit, ed. *Chu Hsi: New Studies.* Honolulu, HI: University of Hawaii Press, 1989.

_____. *Chu Hsi: Life and Thought.* Hong Kong: The Chinese University Press, 1987.

Chan, Wing-tsit. *Chu Hsi and Neo-Confucianism*. Honolulu, HI: University of Hawaii Press, 1986.

_____. "The Evolution of the Neo-Confucian Concept of *li* as Principle." *Tsing Hua Journal of Chinese Studies*, n.s. 4.2 (1964): 123-49.

_____. *A Source Book in Chinese Philosophy*. Princeton, NJ: Princeton University Press, 1963.

_____, tr. *Instructions for Practical Living and Other Neo-Confucian Writings by Wang Yang-ming*. New York: Columbia University Press, 1963.

Chang, Kwang-chih. *Art, Myth and Ritual: The Path to Political Authority in Ancient China*. Cambridge, MA: Harvard University Press, 1983.

_____. *Shang Civilization*. New Haven, CT: Yale University Press, 1980.

Chang, Yü-ch'üan. "Wang Shou-jen as a Statesman." *Chinese Social and Political Science Review,* 23. Reprint. Arlington, VA: University Publications of America, 1975.

Ch'en, Kenneth. *Buddhism in China: A Historical Survey*. Princeton, NJ: Princeton University Press, 1964.

Cheng, Chung-ying, tr. *Tai Chen's Inquiry into Goodness*. Honolulu, HI: East West Center Press, 1969.

Chin, Ann-ping and Mansfield Freeman, trs. *Tai Chen on Mencius: Explorations in Words and Meanings.* New Haven, CT: Yale University Press, 1990.

Ching, Julia. *To Acquire Wisdom: The Way of Wang Yang-ming*. New York: Columbia University Press, 1976.

_____. *The Philosophical Letters of Wang Yang-ming*. Columbia, SC: University of South Carolina Press, 1973.

Cook, Francis H. *Hua-yen Buddhism: The Jewel Net of Indra*. University Park, PA: Pennsylvania State University Press, 1977.

Creel, Herrlee G. *The Origin of Statecraft in China.* Vol. 1. Chicago: University of Chicago Press, 1970.

_____. *Confucius: The Man and the Myth.* New York: John Day Co., 1949.

Csikszentmihalyi, Mark, and Philip J. Ivanhoe, eds. *Religious and Philosophical Aspects of the Laozi.* Albany, NY: SUNY Press, 1998.

Cua, Antonio S. *Ethical Argumentation: A Study in Hsün Tzu's Moral Epistemology.* Honolulu, HI: University of Hawaii Press, 1985.

Darwall, Stephen. "Empathy, Sympathy, Care." *Philosophical Studies,* 89 (1998): 261-82.

De Bary, Wm. Theodore, ed. *Self and Society in Ming Thought.* New York: Columbia University Press, 1970.

_____, ed. *Sources of Chinese Tradition.* Vol. 1. New York: Columbia University Press, 1960.

Demieville, Paul. "Le Miroir Spirituel." *Sinologica,* 1.2 (1947): 112-37.

Dihle, Albrecht. *The Theory of Will in Classical Antiquity.* Berkeley, CA: University of California Press, 1982.

Dubs, Homer H. "Mencius and Sun-dz on Human Nature," *Philosophy East and West,* 6 (1965): 213-22.

Dumoulin, Heinrich. *Zen Buddhism: A History.* Vol. 1. New York: Macmillan Publishing Company, 1988.

Ebrey, Patricia B., tr. *Chu Hsi's Family Rituals: A Twelfth-century Chinese Manual for the Performance of Cappings, Weddings, Funerals, and Ancestral Rites.* Princeton, NJ: Princeton University Press, 1991.

Eliade, Mircea, ed. *The Encyclopedia of Religion.* New York: Macmillan Publishing Co., 1987.

Elman, Benjamin. *From Philosophy to Philology.* Cambridge, MA: Harvard University Press, 1984.

Eno, Robert. *The Confucian Creation of Heaven*. Albany, NY: SUNY Press, 1990.

Erikson, Erik H. *Young Man Luther: A Study in Psychoanalysis and History*. New York: W.W. Norton, 1958.

Ewell, Jr., John W. "Reinventing the Way: Dai Zhen's *Evidential Commentary on the Meaning of Terms in Mencius (1777)*." Berkeley, CA: Unpublished Dissertation in history, 1990.

Fingarette, Herbert. "Response to Hansen's Review," *Journal of Chinese Philosophy*, 7 (1980): 259-66.

_____. "Response to Rosemont's Review," *Philosophy East and West,* 28.4 (October, 1978): 511-14.

_____. *Confucius—The Secular as Sacred.* New York: Harper and Row, 1972.

Foot, Philippa. *Virtues and Vices*. Berkeley, CA: University of California Press, 1978.

Freeman, Mansfield, tr. *Preservation of Learning*. Los Angeles, CA: Monumenta Serica of the University of California, 1972.

_____. "The Philosophy of Tai Tung-yuan," *Journal of the North China Branch of the Royal Asiatic Society*, 64 (1933): 50-71.

_____. "Yen Hsi-chai: A 17th Century Philosopher," *Journal of the North China Branch of the Royal Asiatic Society*, 57 (1926): 70-91.

Fung, Yu-lan. *A History of Chinese Philosophy*. Derk Bodde, tr. Princeton, NJ: Princeton University Press, 1953.

Fussell, Paul. *Class*. New York: Ballantine Books, 1983.

Gallagher, Michael, tr. *Runaway Horses*. New York: Pocket Books, 1975.

Gardiner, Patrick, ed. *Theories of History*. Glencoe, IL: The Free Press, 1959.

Gardner, Daniel K., tr. *Learning to be a Sage*. Berkeley, CA: University of California Press, 1990.

Gimello, Robert M., and Peter N. Gregory, eds. *Studies in Ch'an and Hua-yen*. Honolulu HI: University of Hawaii Press, 1983.

Goldin, Paul. *Rituals of the Way: The Philosophy of Xunzi*. Chicago: Open Court Press, 1999.

Graf, Olaf. *Tao und Jen: Sein und Sollen im sungchinesischen Monismus*. Wiesbaden: Harrassowitz, 1970.

Graham, A.C. *Two Chinese Philosophers*. Reprint. LaSalle, IL: Open Court Press, 1992.

_____. *Disputers of the Tao*. LaSalle, IL: Open Court Press, 1989.

_____. *Later Mohist Logic, Ethics and Science*. Hong Kong: Chinese University Press, 1978.

_____. "The Background of the Mencian Theory of Human Nature." *Tsing Hua Journal of Chinese Studies*, n.s. 6.1-2 (1967): 215-74. Reprinted in *Studies in Chinese Philosophy and Philosophical Literature*. Albany, NY: SUNY Press, 1990.

Gregory, Peter, ed., *Sudden and Gradual: Approaches to Enlightenment in Chinese Thought*. Honolulu, HI: University of Hawaii Press, 1987.

Hacking, Ian. *Why Does Language Matter to Philosophy?* Reprint. Cambridge, MA: Cambridge University Press, 1990.

Hansen, Chad. "Review of *Confucius—the Secular as Sacred*." *Journal of Chinese Philosophy*, 3 (1976): 197-204.

Henderson, John B. *Scripture, Canon, and Commentary: A Comparison of Confucian and Western Exegesis*. Princeton, NJ: Princeton University Press, 1991.

Henke, Frederick Goodrich, tr. *The Philosophy of Wang Yang-ming*. London and Chicago: Open Court Press, 1916. Reprint. New York: Paragon Book Corporation, 1964.

Higgins, Kathleen. *The Music of Our Lives.* Philadelphia, PA: Temple University Press, 1991.

_____. "Music in Confucius and Neo-Confucian Philosophy," *International Philosophical Quarterly*, 20.4 (December, 1980): 433-51.

Huang, Siu-chi. *Lu Hsiang-shan: A Twelfth Century Chinese Idealist Philosopher.* Reprint. Westport, CT: Hyperion Press, 1977.

Hummel, Arthur. *Eminent Chinese of the Ch'ing Period (1644-1911).* 2 vols. Washington, DC: Government Printing Office, 1943-44.

Ihara, Craig K. "David Wong on Emotions in Mencius," *Philosophy East and West*, 41.1 (January, 1991): 45-53.

Irwin, Terence. *Plato's Moral Theory: The Early and Middle Dialogues.* Oxford: Clarendon Press, 1977.

Ivanhoe, Philip J. "Chinese Self-Cultivation and Mencian Extension." *Journal of the History of Ideas* (Forthcoming).

_____, ed. *Chinese Language, Thought, and Culture.* LaSalle, IL: Open Court Press, 1996.

_____. "A Happy Symmetry: Xunzi's Ethical Thought," *Journal of the American Academy of Religion*, 59.2 (Summer, 1991): 309-22.

_____. "Character Consequentialism: An Early Confucian Contribution to Contemporary Ethical Theory," *The Journal of Religious Ethics*, 19.1 (Spring, 1991): 55-70.

_____. "Review of *Thinking Through Confucius*," *Philosophy East and West*, 41.2 (April, 1991): 241-54.

_____. *Ethics in the Confucian Tradition: The Thought of Mencius and Wang Yang-ming.* Atlanta, GA: Scholars Press, 1990.

_____. "Thinking and Learning in Early Confucianism," *Journal of Chinese Philosophy*, 17 (1990): 473-93.

_____. "Reweaving the 'one thread' of the *Analects*," *Philosophy East and West*, 40.1 (January, 1990): 17-33.

Jiang, Xinyan. *Courage, Passion and Virtue.* PhD Dissertation, University of Cincinnati, 1994.

Kant, Immanuel. "Idee zu einter allgemeinen Geschichte in weltburgerlicher Absicht." (1784).

Keightley, David N., ed. *The Origins of Chinese Civilization.* Berkeley: University of California Press, 1983.

_____. *Sources of Shang History: The Oracle-bone Inscriptions of Bronze Age China.* Berkeley, CA: University of California Press, 1978.

King, Sallie B. *Buddha Nature.* Albany, NY: SUNY Press, 1991.

Kline III, T. C., and Philip J. Ivanhoe, eds. *Virtue, Nature, and Moral Agency in the Xunzi.* Indianapolis, IN: Hackett Publishing Co., 2000.

Knoblock, John, tr. *Xunzi: A Translation and Study of the Complete Works.* Vol. 3. Stanford, CA: Stanford University Press, 1994.

_____, tr. *Xunzi: A Translation and Study of the Complete Works.* Vol. 2. Stanford, CA: Stanford University Press, 1990.

_____, tr. *Xunzi: A Translation and Study of the Complete Works.* Vol. 1. Stanford, CA: Stanford University Press, 1988.

_____. "The Chronology of Xunzi's Works." *Early China*, 8 (1982-1983): 29-52.

Kupperman, Joel. *Character.* New York: Oxford University Press, 1991.

Lau, D. C., tr. *The Analects.* New York: Dorset Press, 1979.

_____. "A Note on *ko-wu*," *Bulletin of the School of Oriental and African Studies*, 30 (1967): 535-37.

Legge, James, tr. *The Chinese Classics. Vol. 3. The Shoo King.* Reprint. Hong Kong: Hong Kong University Press, 1970.

_____, tr. *The Chinese Classics. Vol. 4. The She King.* Reprint. Hong Kong: Hong Kong University Press, 1970.

_____, tr. *The Chinese Classics. Vol. 5. The Tso Chuen.* Reprint. Hong Kong: Hong Kong University Press, 1970.

Lewis, Mark Edward. *Writing and Authority in Early China.* Albany, NY: SUNY Press, 1999.

Liang, Ch'i-ch'ao. *Intellectual Trends in the Ch'ing Period.* Immanuel Hsu, tr. Cambridge, MA: Harvard University Press, 1959.

Liu, Xiusheng. *The Place of Humanity in Ethics: Combined Insights from Hume and Mencius.* PhD Dissertation. University of Texas at Austin, December 1999.

Lodén, Torbjörn, tr. "Dai Zhen's Evidential Commentary on the Meaning of the Words of Mencius," *Bulletin of the Museum of Far Eastern Antiquities.* No. 60 (Stockholm, 1988): 165-313.

Lovin, Robin W., and Frank E. Reynolds, eds. *Cosmogony and Ethical Order: New Studies in Comparative Ethics.* Chicago: University of Chicago Press, 1985.

Lowe, Scott. *Mo Tzu's Religious Blueprint for a Chinese Utopia.* Lewiston, ME: Edwin Mellon Press, 1992.

MacIntyre, Alasdair. *Three Rival Versions of Moral Enquiry: Encyclopedia, Genealogy and Tradition.* Notre Dame, IN: University of Notre Dame Press, 1990.

_____. *Whose Justice? Which Rationality?* Notre Dame, IN: University of Notre Dame Press, 1984.

_____. *After Virtue.* Notre Dame, IN: University of Notre Dame Press, 1984.

McDowell, John. "Are Moral Requirements Hypothetical Imperatives?" *Proceedings of the Aristotelian Society,* Supplementary Volume 52 (1978): 13-29.

Mei, Y. P. *Mo-tse, the Neglected Rival of Confucius.* London: Arthur Probsthain, 1934.

_____, tr. *The Ethical and Political Works of Motse.* London: Arthur Probsthain, 1929.

Metzger, Thomas A. *Escape from Predicament.* New York: Columbia University Press, 1977.

Munro, Donald J. *The Concept of Man in Early China.* Stanford, CA: Stanford University Press, 1969.

Nagel, Thomas. *Mortal Questions.* Reprint. London: Cambridge University Press, 1982.

Needham, Joseph. *Science and Civilization in China.* Vol. 2. Cambridge: Cambridge University Press, 1956.

Nivison, David S. *The Ways of Confucianism: Investigations in Chinese Philosophy.* Bryan W. Van Norden, ed. LaSalle, IL: Open Court Press, 1996.

_____. "The Dates of Western Chou," *Harvard Journal of Asiatic Studies,* 43 (1983): 481-580.

_____. "Two Roots or One?" *Proceedings and Addresses of the American Philosophical Association,* 53.6 (August, 1980): 739-61.

_____. "Mencius and Motivation," *Journal of the American Academy of Religion Thematic Issue,* 47.3s (September, 1979): 418-32.

_____. "Royal 'Virtue' in Shang Oracle Inscriptions," *Early China,* 4 (1978-79): 52-55.

_____. "Moral Decision in Wang Yang-ming: The Problem of Chinese 'existentialism'," *Philosophy East and West,* 23.1-2 (1973): 121-38.

_____. *The Life and Thought of Chang Hsüeh-ch'eng 1738-1801.* Stanford, CA: Stanford University Press, 1966.

_____. "Review of *Instructions for Practical Living and Other Neo-Confucian Writings by Wang Yang-ming* by Wing-tsit Chan and *Instructions for Practical Life* by Goodrich Henke," *Journal of the American Oriental Society,* 84.4 (1964): 440-41.

Nussbaum, Martha C. *The Fragility of Goodness.* London: Cambridge University Press, 1986.

O'Neill, Onora, and William Ruddick, eds. *Having Children.* New York: Oxford University Press, 1979.

Pankenier, David W. "Astronomical Dates in Shang and Early Chou," *Early China,* 7 (1981-1982): 2-37.

Pinker, Steven. *The Language Instinct.* Reprint. New York: Harper-Collins Publishers, 1995.

Plato. *Protagoras.* W. K. C. Guthrie, tr. London: Penguin Books, 1979.

_____. *Republic.* G. M. A. Grube, tr., C. D. C. Reeve, rev. Indianapolis, IN: Hackett Publishing Company, 1992.

Rahula, Walpola. *What the Buddha Taught.* Reprint. New York: Grove Press, 1974.

Raphals, Lisa. *Sharing the Light: Women and Virtue in Early China.* Albany, NY: SUNY Press, 1999.

Ropp, Paul S., ed. *Heritage of China.* Berkeley, CA: University of California Press, 1990.

Rorty, Amélie Oksenberg, ed. *Essays on Aristotle's Ethics.* Berkeley, CA: University of California Press, 1980.

Rosemont, Jr., Henry. "Reply to Fingarette's Response," *Philosophy East and West,* 28.4 (October, 1978): 515-19.

_____. "Review of *Confucius—The Secular as Sacred,*" *Philosophy East and West,* 26.4 (October, 1976): 463-77.

*Routledge Encyclopedia of Philosophy.* Vol. 6. London: Routledge Press, 1998.

Ryle, Gilbert. *The Concept of Mind.* London: Hutchinson's University Library, 1949.

Sayre-McCord, Geoffrey, ed. *Essays on Moral Realism.* Ithaca, NY: Cornell University Press, 1988.

Schwartz, Benjamin I. *The World of Thought in Ancient China.* Cambridge, MA: The Belknap Press, 1985.

Shakespeare, William. *King Lear.* Kenneth Muir, ed. London: Methuen and Co., Ltd. 1952.

Shaughnessy, Edward L. *Sources of Western Zhou History: Inscribed Bronze Vessels.* Berkeley, CA: University of California Press, 1991.

Shils, Edward. *Tradition.* Chicago: University of Chicago Press, 1981.

Shun, Kwong-loi. *Mencius and Early Chinese Thought.* Stanford, CA: Stanford University Press, 1997.

_____. "Mencius' Criticism of Mohism: An Analysis of *Meng Tzu* 3A5," *Philosophy East and West,* 41.2 (April, 1991): 203-14.

_____. "Moral Reasons in Confucian Ethics." *Journal of Chinese Philosophy,* 16 (1989): 317-43.

Slingerland, Edward G. "The Conception of *Ming* in Early Chinese Thought," *Philosophy East and West,* 46.4 (1996): 567-81.

Smith, Jonathan Z. "The Influence of Symbols on Social Change: A Place to Stand," *Worship,* 44 (1970): 457-74.

Sommers, Christina H. "Filial Morality," *The Journal of Philosophy,* (1986): 439-56.

Tillman, Hoyt C. *Confucian Discourse and Chu Hsi's Ascendency.* Honolulu, HI: University of Hawaii Press, 1992.

Tocqueville, Alexis de. *Democracy in America.* George Lawrence, tr. J. P. Mayer, ed. New York: Doubleday Anchor Books, 1969.

Tu, Wei-ming, ed. *The Living Tree: The Changing Meaning of Being Chinese Today.* Stanford, CA: Stanford University Press, 1994.

_____. *Centrality and Commonality: An Essay on Confucian Religiousness.* Reprint. Albany, NY: SUNY Press, 1989.

_____, ed. *Humanity and Self-Cultivation: Essays in Confucian Thought.* Berkeley, CA: University of California Press, 1979.

_____. *Neo-Confucian Thought in Action.* Berkeley, CA: University of California Press, 1976.

Van Norden, Bryan W., ed. *Confucius and the Analects: New Essays.* New York: Oxford University Press, 2000.

_____. "Kwong-loi Shun on Moral Reasons in Mencius," *Journal of Chinese Philosophy*, 18 (1991): 353-70.

_____. "Mencius on Courage," in Peter A. French, Theodore E. Uehling, and Howard K. Wettstein, eds. *Midwest Studies in Philosophy.* Vol. 21. Notre Dame, IN: University of Notre Dame Press, 1997, pp. 237-56.

Van Zoeren, Steven. *Poetry and Personality.* Stanford, CA: Stanford University Press, 1991.

Vlastos, Gregory. *Socrates: Ironist and Moral Philosopher.* Ithaca, NY: Cornell University Press, 1991.

Waley, Arthur, tr. *The Analects of Confucius.* New York: Vintage Books, 1938.

Walton, Kendall L. "Projectivism, Empathy and Musical Tension," *Philosophical Topics.* (Forthcoming).

Watson, Burton, tr. *The Complete Works of Chuang Tzu.* New York: Columbia University Press, 1968.

_____, tr. *Mo Tzu: Basic Writings.* New York: Columbia University Press, 1963.

_____, tr. *Hsün Tzu: Basic Writings.* New York: Columbia University Press, 1963.

Williams, Bernard. *Moral Luck.* London: Cambridge University Press, 1986.

Williams, Paul. *Mahāyāna Buddhism: The Doctrinal Foundations.* London: Routledge, 1989.

Wong, David B. "Is There a Distinction between Reason and Emotion in Mencius?" *Philosophy East and West*, 41.1 (January, 1991): 45-53.

_____. "Universalism versus Love with Distinctions: An Ancient Debate Revived," *Journal of Chinese Philosophy.* 16.3, 4 (September-December, 1989): 251-72.

Wright, Arthur. *Buddhism in Chinese History.* Stanford, CA: Stanford University Press, 1959.

_____, ed. *Studies in Chinese Thought.* Chicago: University of Chicago Press, 1953.

Yampolsky, Phillip B., tr. *The Platform Sutra of the Sixth Patriarch.* New York: Columbia University Press, 1967.

Yearley, Lee H. *Mencius and Aquinas: Theories of Virtue and Conceptions of Courage.* Albany, NY: SUNY Press, 1990.

_____. "Teachers and Saviors," *The Journal of Religion,* 65.2 (April, 1985): 225-43.

Yü, Ying-shih. "Tai Chen's Choice between Philosophy and Philology," *Asia Major,* n.s. 2.1 (1989): 79-108.

_____. "Some Preliminary Observations on the Rise of Ch'ing Confucian Intellectualism," *Tsing Hua Journal of Chinese Studies,* 11 (1975): 101-46.

# Name Index

Allan, Sarah, 25
Ames, Roger T., 8
Aquinas, Saint Thomas, 43
Aristotle, ix, 43, 71
Augustine, Saint, 31-32, 39-40, 62, 64, 71

Bao Si, xi, xv
Bellah, Robert, 88
Berkson, Mark, 55
Bodde, Derk, 23, 73, 84
Bol, Peter K., 54
Brooks, Bruce E. and Taeko A., 8
Bruce, J. Percy, 54
Buddha, 91
Burnyeat, M. F., 71

Cang Jie, 86
Chan, Wing-tsit, 23, 54-58, 69, 71-73, 97-98
Chang, K. C., xiv, 86
Chang Yü-chüan, 70
Ch'en, Kenneth, 55
Cheng, Chung-ying, 98
Cheng Yi, 43, 50, 55, 58, 62
Chin, Ann-ping, 98
Ching, Julia, 57, 67-70
Cook, Francis H., 56
Creel, Herrlee G., xv, 8
Csikszentmihalyi, Mark, xvi
Cua, Antonio S., 39

Darwall, Stephen, 25
De Bary, Wm. Theodore, 56, 72, 98
Demieville, Paul, 56
Dihle, Albrecht, 71
Dubs, Homer H., 31-32, 39
Dumoulin, Heinrich, 55

Ebrey, Patricia B., 85
Einstein, Albert, 19
Eliade, Mircea, xv, 24-25
Elman, Benjamin, 85, 87, 97
English, Jane, xvi
Eno, Robert, 24
Erikson, Erik H., 69
Ewell Jr., John W., 98

Fingarette, Herbert, 10-11
Foot, Philippa, 12
Freeman, Mansfield, 84-88, 97-98
Freud, Sigmund, 41
Fu Xi, 86
Fu Yue, 70
Fung Yu-lan, 23, 84, 87, 97
Fussell, Paul, 13

Gallagher, Michael, 71
Gandhi, Mahatma, xiii
Gardiner, Patrick, 41
Gardner, Daniel K., 54
Gimello, Robert M., 56
Goldin, Paul, 38
Gongduzi, 20
Graf, Olaf, 55
Graham, A. C., 23-24, 55, 72
Gregory, Peter, 56
Guthrie, W. K. C., 71

Hacking, Ian, 41
Hall, David H., 8
Han Yü, 30, 91, 98
Hansen, Chad, 11
Henderson, John B., 54
Henke, Goodrich, 72-73
Higgins, Kathleen, 13

118

Hobbes, Thomas, 41
Hsu, Immanuel, 85
Huang Di, 83-84, 86, 88
Huang Siu-chi, 58
Hummel, Arthur, 85, 97
Hutton, Eric L., 12, 86

Ihara, Craig, 26
Irwin, Terence, 14, 71

Jiang Xinyan, 26

Kant, Immanuel, 36, 41
Keightley, David N., xiv
Kierkegaard, Søren, 72
King Jr., Martin Luther, xiii
King, Sallie B., 55
Kline III, T. C., 10, 12, 24, 38-40
Knoblock, John, 38, 86
Kupperman, Joel, 12, 14, 39

Lancefield, Betsy, 73
Laozi, 91
Lau, D. C., 10, 24-25, 39, 58
Lawrence, George, 88
Legge, James, xiv-xvii, 57, 70, 87
Lewis, Mark E., 86
Liang, Ch'i-ch'ao, 85
Ling, Derek Fung, 39
Liu Xiusheng, 24-25
Lodén, Torbjörn, 98
Lovin, Robin W., 9
Lowe, Scott, 23
Lu Xiangshan, 51, 58

MacIntyre, Alasdair, 38-39
Mao Tse-tung, 70
Mayer, J. P., 88
McDowell, John, 38-39
Mei, Y. P., 23
Metzger, Thomas A., 55

Mishima, Yukio, 61
Mozi, 15-16, 23, 43, 91
Muir, Kenneth, 72
Munro, Donald J., xiv, xvii

Nagel, Thomas, 37, 58
Needham, Joseph, 23
Nivison, David S., xiv-xv,
    23-26, 70-73, 86-87
Nussbaum, Martha C., 38

Oates, Whitney J., 40
Okada Takehiko, 72
O'Neill, Onora, xvi

Pankenier, David W., xv
Pinker, Steven, 27
Plato, 13-14, 57, 71

Qi Bo, 84, 88

Rahula, Walpola, 55
Raphals, Lisa, xv
Reynolds, Frank E., 9
Ropp, Paul S., xiv
Rorty, Amélie Oksenberg, 71
Rosemont Jr., Henry, 11, 26,
    40
Ruddick, William, xvi
Ryle, Gilbert, 71

Sayre-McCord, Geoffrey, 39
Schofer, Jon W., 40
Schwartz, Benjamin I., 10-
    11, 23
Scott, William C., 71
Shakespeare, William, 72
Shaughnessy, Edward L.,
    xiv
Shen Nong, 86
Shils, Edward, 38

Shun, Kwong-loi, 23-24, 26
Shun (Sage King), xvi, 27, 86
Sima Guang, 58
Sima Qian, xv
Slingerland, Edward G., xv
Smith, Jonathan Z., 8
Sommers, Christina H., xvi
Socrates, 15, 61-62, 64, 74
Sorabji, Richard, 71
Sterling, Richard W., 71

Tang (Sage King), 27
Tillman, Hoyt C., 54
Tocqueville, Alexis de, 84, 88
Tu, Wei-ming, xvii, 69, 85

Van Norden, Bryan W., xiv, 8, 10, 14,
    26, 39, 72
Van Zoeren, Steven, 10, 12
Vlastos, Gregory, 13

Waley, Arthur, xv, 10-11
Walton, Kendall L., 13
Wang Xianqian, 30-31, 39
Watson, Burton, xvi, 11, 23-24, 39-42,
    56, 98

Wen (King), 9
Williams, Bernard, 38
Williams, Paul, 55-56
Wilson, Stephen H., 12
Wong, David B., 23, 26, 40
Wright, Arthur, 55, 71
Wu (Sage King), 27

Xu Ai, 67-68
Xuan (King), 18-19, 22, 98

Yampolsky, Phillip B., 56
Yan Hui, 5, 6, 9
Yang Zhu, 15-16, 24, 43, 91
Yao (Sage King), xvi, 27, 86
Yearley, Lee H., 9, 26, 72
Yi Yin, 27
Yi Zhi, 23
Yü (Sage King), 79, 86
Yü, Ying-shih, 58, 85, 98

Zhang Shiqing, 78
Zhang Xuecheng, 85-88
Zhuangzi, 45-46, 91
Zigong, 3, 9, 10

# Subject Index

acquisition model, 8, 101

agricultural metaphors, 20, 25, 27, 29, 33, 36, 60

always work at self cultivation. See *biyou shi yan*

archery, 5, 79, 82, 86

*bao* 報 ("repay"), ix, xii

benevolence. See *ren*

*benxing* 本性 ("original nature"), 46, 48, 56. See also *tianming zhi xing*

*biran* 必然 ("necessary"), 93, 95-96

*biyou shi yan* 必有事焉 ("always work at self cultivation"), 65

*bo* 博 ("breadth"), 51

breadth, See *bo*

Buddha-nature, 45-46, 55

Buddhism, ix, 43-46, 54-56, 59-60, 70, 75, 79-80, 82-83, 91, 95, 97, 101-103

*buyi zhi ze* 不易之則 ("unchanging standard"), 92-93, 95-96

*cai* 才 ("capacity" or "talent"), 47

capacity. See *cai*

*Chan* 禪 ("Zen"), 45, 55, 57, 82, 87

*changzhi* 常知 ("ordinary knowledge"), 62, 63, 66

*Changes*. See *Yijing*

*cheng* 誠 ("sincerity" "integrity"), 60, 64-65, 67, 72

*chengyi* 誠意 ("making one's thoughts sincere"), 50-51

Cheng-Zhu School, 58, 75, 79, 81

*Chuanxilu* 傳習錄, 67, 70, 73

*Chunqiu* 春秋 (*Spring and Autumn Annals*), 50, 77

character (moral), x-xi, 2, 4, 6-7, 9, 12-13, 47

classics, 1-2, 49-53, 58, 65, 68-69, 75-79, 81, 83, 86, 89-92, 95-97, 102-103

clue. See *xu*

compassion, 45, 64, 66

courage, 6, 12, 20, 26, 64, 66

cultivated person. See *junzi*

culture. See *wen*

*cunxin* 存心 ("preserving the mind"), 49, 57, 82

*Cunxue bian* 存學編 (*Preserving Learning*), 86-88

*Cunxing bian* 存性編 (*Preserving Nature*), 87

*Daodejing* 道德經, 11

*dao wenxue* 道問學 ("pursuing inquiry and study"), 49, 52, 57, 82

Daoism, ix, xvi, 43-44, 46, 56, 59, 70, 75, 85, 91, 95, 97, 102-103

*daoxin* 道心 ("mind of the Way"), 48, 57

*Daxue* 大學 (*Great Learning*), 50, 54, 63

*de* 得 ("to get"), ix

*de* 德 ("virtue" "moral charisma"), ix-xvii, 2, 58

deliberate action. See *wei*

destiny. See *ming* 命

developmental model, 29, 33, 36, 40, 101

*ding* 定 ("meditative calm"), 57

discovery model, 60, 102

*Doctrine of the Mean*. See *Zhongyong*

*duan* 端 ("moral sprouts"), 18-22, 24-25, 33, 37, 46, 56, 59-60, 94, 99

egoism, 16
emptiness, 44-45
energy. See *qi*
enlightenment, 52, 56, 60, 70, 73, 80
Erudites. See *ru*
etiquette, 4-5, 11-12, 69
examinations (civil service), 52, 54
existentialism, 67, 72-73
extension. See *tui*

*Family Ritual*. See *Jiali*
Farmer of Song, 21, 25
filial piety. See *xiao*
Five Classics. See *Wujing*
flood-like energy. See *haoran zhi qi*
Four Books. See *Sishu*

*geming* 革命 ("revolution"), xv
get. See *de* 得
*gewu* 格物 ("investigation of things"), 49-50, 81
golden rule, 8, 14, 93-97, 99
grasp of the essential. See *yue*
*Great Learning*. See *Daxue*

*Han Changli quanji* 韓昌黎全集, 39, 98
Han (dynasty), 50, 72-79
*haoran zhi qi* 浩然之氣 ("flood-like energy"), 20, 26, 56
heart. See *xin*
Heaven. See *tian*
Heavenly endowed nature. See *Tianming zhi xing*
hedonism, 24

*Henan Chengshi yishu* 河南程氏遺書, 71
history (role in self cultivation) 50, 52-53, 92, 96
*History*. See *Shujing*
honoring the virtuous nature. See *zun dexing*
*Huayan* (Buddhist School), 56
*hui* 慧 ("insight"), 57
human mind. See *renxin*
human nature. See *renxing*
humanity. See *ren*

incipient tendencies, xii, 1, 5, 16, 22, 24, 29, 36, 46
Indra's Net, 56
insight. See *hui*
integrity. See *cheng*
intuition. See moral intuition
investigation of things. See *gewu*

*Jiali* 家禮 (*Family Ritual*), 75
*jing* 敬 ("reverence"), x-xiii, xvi, 2, 49, 52, 57-58, 82, 87
*jingzuo* 靜坐 ("quiet sitting"), 49, 57, 80, 83, 89, 92
*junzi* 君子 ("cultivated person"), xiii-xiv, xvii, 5, 13, 38

*King Lear*, 72
know-how, 2, 9, 71, 82, 84
knowledge and action, 51, 61-64, 72, 82

language empiricists, 34, 41
language innatists, 34, 41
learning. See *xue*
*Laozi* 老子, xvi
*li* 理 ("principle" "pattern"), 46-53, 56-57, 59, 72, 79-81, 83, 87, 92-95, 102

*li* 禮 ("rites" "rituals"), xi, xv, 1-13, 16, 32-35, 38, 75-77, 79, 81-82, 92
*liangzhi* 良知 ("pure knowing"), 68, 79, 102
*lihui* 理會 ("to understand"), 57
*Liji* 禮記 (*Rites*), 50, 77
*Liujing* 六經 ("Six Classics"), 95
*Liuyi* 六藝 ("Six Arts"), 79, 86-87
Lord on High. See *Shang Di*
Lu-Wang School, 50, 58, 75

making one's thoughts sincere. See *chengyi*
Manchus, 76, 81
Mandate of Heaven. See *Tianming*
material nature. See *qizhi zhi xing*
medicine (as metaphor for moral learning), 67, 83-84, 88
meditative calm. See *ding*
*meng* 萌 ("sprouts"), 22, 25
*Mengzi ziyi shuzheng* 孟子字義疏證, 91-92, 98
metaphysics, 44, 49, 55-56, 58-59, 76, 79-80, 103
*miao* 苗 ("sprouts"), 25
mind. See *xin*
mind of the Way. See *daoxin*
mindful practice. See *yixingsanmei*
*ming* 命 ("orders" "destiny"), x-xi
mirror as metaphor, 34, 45-46, 56, 63, 68, 70-71
Mohists, 15-17, 23
moral charisma. See *de* 德
moral intuition, 10, 14, 35, 37, 49, 51-53, 69, 96, 99. See also *duan* and *liangzhi*
moral luck, 29, 37
moral psychology, 15, 26, 59, 62
moral sprouts. See *duan*
*Mozi* 墨子, xvi, 15-17, 23, 43, 91

music, 6-7, 12-13, 15, 38, 79, 82-84, 86

natural. See *ziran*
necessary. See *biran*
*Nicomachean Ethics*, 71
*nie* 櫱 ("sprouts"), 22

*Odes*. See *Shijing*
opinion. See *yijian*
orders. See *ming* 命
ordinary knowledge. See *changzhi*
original nature. See *benxing*

pattern. See *li*
philology, 89-92, 95, 97-98
*Platform Sutra*, 45, 56-57, 70
Platonic Forms, 57
practice. See *xi*
praxis model, 81-82, 102
*Preserving Learning*. See *Cunxue bian*
*Preserving Nature*. See *Cunxing bian*
preserving the mind. See *cunxin*
*principle*. See *li*
*Protagoras*, 71
pure knowing. See *liangzhi*
pursuing inquiry and study. See *dao wenxue*

*qi* 氣 ("energy"), 20, 26, 47-49, 56-57, 79-80, 87
Qin (dynasty), 23, 68, 78
Qing (dynasty), 76, 85, 89, 102
*qizhi zhi xing* 氣質之性 ("material nature"), 48, 80
quiet sitting. See *jingzuo*
quietism, 49, 65

real knowledge. See *zhenzhi*

realization model, 94, 103
recovery model, 46, 49, 102
reflection. See *si*
re-formation model, 32-33, 36, 40, 101
*ren* 仁 ("humanity" "benevolence"), xvi, 5-6, 11, 18, 24-25, 37, 48, 57, 91
*renxin* 人心 ("human mind"), 48
*renxing* 人性 ("human nature"), 9, 12, 15-20, 22, 24-25, 27, 29-33, 35-36, 40-41, 43-46, 48-49, 52, 55-60, 72, 78-81, 101-102. See also *xing'e* and *xingshan*
repay. See *bao*
*Republic*, 13, 71
reverence. See *jing*
revolution. See *geming*
rites. See *li*
*Rites*. See *Liji*
rituals. See *li*
*ru* 儒 ("Erudites"), 8

sages, xvi, 1-2, 6, 9, 27, 30, 32-38, 46, 53, 68-69, 71, 75, 77-79, 82-83, 86, 90-91, 96-97
second nature, 1, 36, 60, 101
self deception, 18, 60-61
selfish (desires, thoughts, opinions), xi, 24, 45, 60-61, 63-68, 79, 94, 103
*Shang Di* 上帝 ("The Lord on High"), x
Shang (dynasty), ix, xi, xiv
*Shao* (Dance), 6, 13
*Shao Nan*, 79
*Shiji* 史記 (*Records of the Historian*), xv
*Shijing* 詩經 (*Odes*), xvi, 3-4, 7, 9-10, 13, 18-19, 36, 42, 50, 77, 79, 87

*Shishuo* 師説, 97-98
*shu* 恕 ("sympathetic understanding"), 98
*Shujing* 書經 (*History*), xii, xv-xvi, 50, 57, 70
*si* 思 ("reflection "), 2-3, 9-10, 20, 26, 29, 37, 96
*Sikuquanshu* 四庫全書, 89
sincerity. See *cheng*
*Sishu* 四書 ("Four Books"), 50
*Sishujizhu* 四書集注, 56
*Sishuzhengwu* 四書正誤, 85-87
Six Arts. See *Liuyi*
Six Classics. See *Liujing*
Song (dynasty), 30, 44, 50, 54, 75-80, 83, 87, 95, 102
sprouts. See *duan, meng, miao, nie*
*Spring and Autumn Annals*. See *Chunqiu*
sympathetic understanding. See *shu*

talent. See *cai*
Tang (dynasty), 30
Ten Commandments, 11
therapy (philosophy as), 61, 64, 66-68
*tian* 天 (" Heaven "), x-xii, xv, xvii, 9, 16-18, 20-22, 24-25, 27, 35, 47-48, 80, 90, 92, 95
*Tianming* 天命 ("Mandate of Heaven "), x, xi, xv
*Tianming zhi xing* 天命之性 ("Heavenly endowed nature"), 80. See also *benxing*
*Treatise on the Golden Lion*, 56
*tui* 推 ("extension"), 20

understand. See *lihui*
unchanging standard. See *buyi zhi ze*

virtue. See *de* 德

*Wangwenchenggong quanshu* 王文
成公全書, 73
Way. See *Dao*
weakness of will, 62
*wen* 文 ("culture" "writing"), 78-
79, 86-87
*wei* 偽 ("deliberate action"), 33, 40
women, xv, xvii
writing. See *wen*
*Wujing* 五經 ("Five Classics"), 50

*xi* 習 ("practice"), 1-2, 4, 6-9, 11,
13, 16, 34-35, 40, 59-60, 62,
69, 76-89, 92, 102
Xia (dynasty), 79, 86
*xiao* 孝 ("filial piety"), xii, xvi, 2,
27, 63-64
*xin* 心 ("heart" "mind"), 11, 18-
20, 22, 25-26, 29, 38, 43-46,
48-49, 52-53, 56-57, 60-61, 63-
72, 78-79, 82-83, 86, 92, 94-95,
99, 102, 104
*xing* 性. See *renxing*
*xing'e* 性惡 ("human nature is
bad"), 12, 30, 32, 39
*xingshan* 性善 ("human nature is
good"), 12, 17-22, 24-25
*xu* 緒 ("clue"), 46, 56

*xue* 學 ("learning"), 1-2, 8-10, 32,
37, 41-42, 49-53, 58, 68, 77-79,
81-82, 91, 96
*Xunzi jijie* 荀子集解, 30

*Yan Yuanji* 顏元記, 85-88
*yijian* 意見 ("opinion"), 92-95
*Yijing* 易經 (*Changes*), 50, 77, 79,
86,
Yin (dynasty). See Shang
*yixingsanmei* 一行三昧 ("mindful
practice"), 57
Yuan (dynasty), 78
*Yuanshan* 原善, 89-91
*yue* 約 ("a grasp of the essential"),
51

Zen. See *Chan*
*zhenzhi* 真知 ("real knowledge"),
62-64, 66
*Zhongyong* 中庸 (*Doctrine of the
Mean*), 50, 54, 57, 85
Zhou (dynasty), x-xv, 76
*Zhou Nan*, 79, 87
*Zhuangzi* 莊子, 11, 24, 56, 91
*ziran*, 自然 ("natural"), 93
*zun dexing* 尊德性 ("honoring the
virtuous nature"), 49, 52
*Zuozhuan* 左傳, xii-xvi